Dr. Cassundra White-Elliott

365 Days
of
Encouragement

909.315.3161
www.clfpublishing.org

Cover Design by Senir Design. Contact information-info@senirdesign.com.

ISBN # 978-0-9899408-4-9

Printed in the United States of America.

Introduction

The purpose of this book is to assist you in walking in the very peace of God. At times, we as believers can become discouraged. We must war against the spirit of the enemy with the Word of God and declare our own encouragement in an effort to overcome discouragement.

Just as our brain requires oxygen obtained from the air we breathe to sustain our mortal bodies, our spirit requires revitalization and encouragement in order to be strengthened each and every day of our lives. The revitalization and encouragement needed for the spirit of man comes directly from the Word of God and assists us in walking according to the way of our heavenly Father.

365 Days of Encouragement provides a scripture a day for each day of the year. Along with the daily scripture is a brief note of commentary also for the benefit of edifying the saints of God.

It is my prayer that the people of God would live a fulfilled life through Christ Jesus. Knowing His Word and understanding we can walk in the fulfillment thereof is empowering. We are instructed in II Timothy 2:15, *"Study to shew thyself approved unto God, a workman that needeth not to be ashamed, rightly dividing the word of truth"* (KJV). Take an opportunity to delve further into the Word of God, to know His statutes and to allow your own personal life to be edified, so you can be equipped to bring glory to God and lived a fulfilled life.

Be blessed,

Dr. C. White-Elliott

See pg. 376 for Bible version abbreviation explanations.

Day 1

*A*s we go along life's journey, it is not very difficult to become discouraged by the occurrences of life itself. At times, our self-image, our character or even our integrity may be called into question. Many may question who we are and our worth, but Psalm 8:3-9 reassures us and reaffirms us.

God created mankind above all created beings. He positioned us a little lower than the angels. Thus, we are valuable in the sight of God. Therefore, we should value one another and ourselves.

Psalm 8:3-9 NIV

When I consider your heavens, the work of your fingers, the moon and the stars, which you have set in place, what is mankind that you are mindful of them, human beings that you care for them? You have made them a little lower than the angels and crowned them with glory and honor. You made them rulers over the works of your hands; you put everything under their feet: all flocks and herds, and the animals of the wild, the birds in the sky, and the fish in the sea, all that swim the paths of the seas.

Day 2

II Peter 1:3 KJV

According as his divine power hath given unto us all things that pertain unto life and godliness, through the knowledge of him that hath called us to glory and virtue.

*L*ife can be likened to a bed of roses. It is filled with sweet fragrances and indescribable beauty. At the same time, there are prickly obstacles that often come to test our faith and may even cause us to question God's involvement in our life. II Peter 1:3 tells us, God has provided for us all things we need for this life and godliness, including diligence, virtue, knowledge, temperance, patience, brotherly kindness, and love (v. 5-7).

Day 3

*W*e as humans are incapable of doing everything we need to do with our limited human strength, whether it is physical strength, emotional

> **Philippians 4:13 KJV**
>
> *I can do all things through Christ which strengtheneth me.*

strength, psychological strength, etc. But in Christ, we are supplied with the appropriate measure of strength we need to accomplish those tasks that seem to present a challenge for us. In Him, there isn't any task too difficult that we are unable to accomplish. We must always remember- In Him, we live; in Him, we move; and, in Him, we have our being!

*H*ave faith in who God has called you to be. Many doubt the very gifts and talents God has placed in them to use to fulfill a specific task. They ask themselves if they can fulfill their hearts' burning desires. If God called you to do something, He will give you what is needed to fulfill the task.

Day 4

> **Romans 8:28-31 KJV**
>
> *And we know that all things work together for good to them that love God, to them who are the called according to his purpose. For whom he did foreknow, he also did predestinate to be conformed to the image of his Son, that he might be the firstborn among many brethren. Moreover whom he did predestinate, them he also called: and whom he called, them he also justified: and whom he justified, them he also glorified. What shall we then say to these things? If God be for us, who can be against us?*

We often question why things happen to us, and we sometimes fail to see the necessity of certain events in our lives. But we must be wise enough to acknowledge the fact that nothing happens to us without God knowing about it. Therefore, if God allows it to occur, there must be a reason.

These instances are opportunities to exercise our faith in God. We must lean not to our own understanding, but hold fast to Romans 8:28-31 that clearly tells us that each event works together. Our life is not lived as isolated events. They fit together as one giant puzzle and something good is coming out of it- if you allow God's will to be done in your life.

Day 5

*W*hether we experience times of joy or times of pain, our Lord and Savior Jesus Christ will be with us every step of the way. When He departed from this earthly realm, He said He must go, but He would send another comforter: the Holy Spirit. The Holy Spirit is our guide. He keeps us on the straight and narrow path. He comforts us. He teaches us. He

> **Hebrews 13:5 KJV**
>
> *Let your conversation be without covetousness; and be content with such things as ye have: for he hath said, I will never leave thee, nor forsake thee.*

speaks to us. He is our present help in our times of trouble. He will never leave or forsake us.

Day 6

> **I Samuel 15:22 NLT**
>
> *But Samuel replied, "What is more pleasing to the LORD: your burnt offerings and sacrifices or your obedience to his voice? Listen! Obedience is better than sacrifice, and submission is better than offering the fat of rams.*

Blessed be the name of the Lord! Each day, we have choices we must make- on our jobs, in our personal lives, while out in society, and when dealing with our families. At times in life, we are challenged to sacrifice our belief system for that which we hope to attain in this world system. When we sacrifice our moral standards, there is a God-given principal to which we are disobedient. However, when we honor the Word of God, we remain in right standing with Him, and for this, we will be rewarded.

Day 7

Christ teaches by example as well as by doctrine. And, for this purpose He came into this world and lived among us, so that He

> **John 13:15 KJV**
>
> *For I have given you an example, that ye should do as I have done to you.*

might set for us an example of all those graces and duties, which the written Word of God teaches. He is a logos lived and walked out, without one false stroke. By His living example, He made His own laws more intelligible and honorable.

Day 8

> **II Timothy 1:7 KJV**
>
> *For God hath not given us the spirit of fear; but of power, and of love, and of a sound mind.*

The spirit of fear comes to grip our hearts and immobilize us. God did not intend for us to be subjected to this demonic influence.

II Timothy 1:7 clearly states, God equipped us with power, love and a sound mind. We must use the power we have to extinguish the fiery darts of the enemy, one being the dart of fear. The only type of fear we should have in our lives is the fear of the Lord God. This fear is reverence for the only true living God.

Day 9

*W*e were born into sin and shaped in iniquity. We are only made perfect in Him, the Son of God. Knowing this, we should not carry the attitude that we have arrived. We should forever be striving for perfection, by keeping our focus on God. Also, we should not focus on the past. Believing we have arrived or being fixated on the past will cause us to miss the present and the prize of the high calling of God in Christ Jesus.

> **Philippians 3:13-14 KJV**
>
> *Brethren, I count not myself to have apprehended: but this one thing I do, forgetting those things which are behind, and reaching forth unto those things which are before, I press toward the mark for the prize of the high calling of God in Christ Jesus.*

Day 10

> **Mark 12:30-31 NIV**
>
> *Love the Lord your God with all your heart and with all your soul and with all your mind and with all your strength.' The second is this: 'Love your neighbor as yourself.' There is no commandment greater than these."*

The Lord our God is one Lord. If we firmly believe this, then we shall love Him with all our heart. He is Jehovah, who has all amiable perfections in Himself; He is our God, to whom we stand related and obliged; therefore, we ought to love Him, to set our affections on Him, and take delight in Him. If He is one Lord, our hearts must be one with Him, and because there is no God besides, no rival must be admitted with Him upon the throne. The second great commandment is to love our neighbor as ourselves, as truly and sincerely as we love ourselves, and in the same instances, and we must show it by doing unto others as we would like done unto us. Our neighbor and we are of one body, of one society, that of the world of mankind. For a fellow Christian, of the same sacred society, the obligation is even stronger.

Day 11

II Chronicles 7:14 is a heavenly plea from God, the creator, to His creation- mankind. It is a recipe for success and a way out of the trouble our world currently faces. If we follow the steps of the recipe explicitly, we will get what we desire: a healed land free from

> **II Chronicles 7:14 KJV**
>
> *If my people, which are called by my name, shall humble themselves, and pray, and seek my face, and turn from their wicked ways; then will I hear from heaven, and will forgive their sin, and will heal their land.*

turmoil and true peace. God is looking for true repentance and humility from His people. He wants us to cry out to Him, seeking His face, not His hands. When and only when we do this will our land be healed.

Day 12

> **Romans 8:31 ESV**
>
> *What then shall we say to these things? If God is for us, who can be against us?*

Our Lord is the greatest advocate we could ever have. He has already defeated Satan, our adversary. So, with the all-powerful God on our side, we don't have to worry about anyone who opposes us. We already have the victory in Him.

Day 13

The mission of our Lord and the mission of Satan are diametrically opposed.

Satan, our adversary, walks the earth as a roaring lion, seeking whom he can devour. He desires to sift us as wheat. He does not want to see us prosper, flourish, or succeed. He wants to wipe

> **John 10:10 KJV**
>
> *The thief cometh not, but for to steal, and to kill, and to destroy: I am come that they might have life, and that they might have it more abundantly.*

us out and render us helpless. However, Jesus, our Lord and Savior, wants us to have an abundant life, filled with the blessings of God. He wants us to be complete in Him, while Satan wants to tear us asunder and cause us to lack and be empty. Given these opposing objectives, which do you want for your life? Whose team are you on?

Day 14

> **Matthew 7:7 NASB**
>
> *Ask, and it will be given to you; seek, and you will find; knock, and it will be opened to you.*

*A*sk, and it will be given. Seek, and you shall find. God has provided the simplest of instructions, but we fail to do our part and follow the instructions, yet we expect the best. God's Word tells us to ask, but pride keeps our mouths closed. When we fail to ask, we fail to obtain. But, when we come before the Lord with a pure heart (with the right motives), He will not withhold any good thing from us.

Day 15

*W*hen we obey the commandments of the Lord, He is obligated by His own words to bless us. All our needs will be supplied when we are obedient to

> **Philippians 4:19 KJV**
>
> *But my God shall supply all your need according to his riches in glory by Christ Jesus.*

what God has told us to do. God is not a man that He should lie. Whatsoever He promises will be done. But, we must first do what we have been commanded and then God will perform His Word with signs following.

Day 16

Lamentations 3:22-23 KJV

*It is of the LORD'S mercies that we are not consumed, because his compassions fail not. **They are** new every morning: great **is** thy faithfulness.*

The god we serve is a compassionate loving god. It is not His desire for us to perish or lose hope.

Therefore, He replenishes His mercies for us each and every morning. Mercy is the unmerited, undeserved, unearned favor of God. We don't deserve it, but we have it. For this cause, we need not to worry, fear, or faint. We need to graciously accept His loving kindness and walk in His mercy. God is just and faithful.

Day 17

*I*n Christ, we have power to face and overcome any trial or snare the enemy presents to us. Our adversary is a defeated foe; however, if we relinquish our power to Satan, we will become defeated too. Instead, we should us the power God granted unto us when we face fiery darts, so they may be quenched.

II Corinthians 2:11 tells us, "We are not ignorant of Satan's

> **Luke 10:19 KJV**
>
> *Behold, I give unto you power to tread on serpents and scorpions, and over all the power of the enemy: and nothing shall by any means hurt you.*

devices;" however, we tend to turn a blind eye or a deaf ear to Satan's tricks and to the Holy Spirit's forewarnings. These behaviors will cause us to be overtaken by Satan. However, this is not the will of God. If it were, He would not have equipped us. If we use the tools we have been supplied with, all will be well.

Day 18

> **Matthew 6:33 KJV**
>
> *But seek ye first the kingdom of God, and his righteousness; and all these things shall be added unto you.*

We at times become side-tracked and consumed with the cares of this world, and lose sight of what is really important- the Lord, His kingdom, and saving the lost. We focus on our careers and career advancement; we focus on our education and obtaining certificates and degrees; we focus on our finances and earning more and more money; we focus on our bodies, so we can stay physically fit and attractive. None of these things are negative in and of themselves. However, if we place these things above seeking God, we have not properly prioritized our lives. God's kingdom and His righteousness must be first and foremost in our lives. When we make God the priority, everything else will fall into place.

Day 19

*I*f it is our testimony that we are servants of the Lord God, we must be found true to our word. A true servant is faithful in his/her calling.

> **I Corinthians 4:2 KJV**
> *Moreover it is required in stewards, that a man be found faithful.*

When we accept an assignment, we must be steadfast and unmovable in the completion of the assignment. Our acceptance of the assignment came from our love of the Lord and our obedience to Him. It was not based on our feelings. Therefore, we should not allow our feelings to dictate whether or not we will continue to see the assignment to completion. God's Word tells us for our Nay to be Nay and our Yea to be Yea. So, if we submit and commit, we must complete!

Day 20

Galatians 5:22-23 NIV

But the fruit of the Spirit is love, joy, peace, forbearance, kindness, goodness, faithfulness, gentleness and self-control. Against such things there is no law.

As followers of Christ, we must detach ourselves from being moved by our flesh and learn to move by the spirit of God and in the fruit of the spirit. We need to replace hatred, envy, strife, unforgiveness, jealousy, back-biting, covetousness, etc. with love, joy, peace, forbearance, kindness, goodness, faithfulness, gentleness, and self-control. God is a rewarder of those who diligently seek Him. When we seek Him, we will obtain the fruit of the spirit, and they will be manifested in our lives.

Day 21

Because God loves us uncon-
ditionally, cares for our overall
well-being, and wishes that
none of us will perish, He
draws us with loving kindness.
It is His desire that we would
all come unto Him.

Once we come, He will
continue to love us because He
has an everlasting love for us.

Jeremiah 31:3 KJV

The LORD hath appeared of old unto me, saying, Yea, I have loved thee with an everlasting love: therefore with lovingkindness have I drawn thee.

Question- Is your love returned to Him? If so, how do you
demonstrate it towards Him and towards others? This is a
thought to ponder today.

Day 22

> **Psalm 119:11 NLT**
>
> *I have hidden your word in my heart, that I might not sin against you.*

From one day to the next, believers, who love God intently, struggle with having their lives line up with God's Word and finding to how replace unrighteous living with righteous living. Psalm 119:11 gives us a key to this dilemma. If we read and meditate on God's Word, we will be able to do God's Word. Psalm 119:11 tells us if we hide God's Word in our heart, we will not sin against Him (by living unrighteously). In order to keep His Word in our heart, we must first know His Word. To know His Word, we must read His Word and continuously be in fellowship with Him.

Day 23

*I*n our human efforts, we constantly face failure. God, though, does not experience failure. There is nothing He has ever done at which He has failed. He is the epitome of success.

> **Jeremiah 32:27 ESV**
>
> *Behold, I am the LORD, the God of all flesh. Is anything too hard for me?*

Note- Just because we do not agree or understand all God has done does not mean He has not succeeded. While we humans may find certain tasks difficult, nothing is too hard for God. All He has to do is speak and the world or a situation will change.

Day 24

Luke 1:37 KJV

For with God nothing shall be impossible.

*I*saiah 55:8 states, *"My thoughts are not your thoughts, nor are my ways your ways."* There are many things we cannot fathom with our human minds. As a result, we cannot move from a non-thought to a product or to an action. We even have trouble moving from an actual idea/thought to an action. However, because God is omnipotent, He can do all things that come to His mind. Nothing is impossible for the one sovereign God.

Day 25

*T*hroughout our lifetime, people will make us promises time and time again. At times, they will follow through; while at other times, they will fall short. When they fall short, they feed us

Luke 18:27 KJV

The things which are impossible with men are possible with God.

excuses and may or may not apologize. Apparently, one of the hardest things for a person to admit is failure or the inability to complete a task, regardless of the reason. Luke 18:27 gives us hope. Man may not be able to deliver, but the one true living God, the omnipotent God, can.

Day 26

> **Proverbs 3:5-6 KJV**
>
> *Trust in the LORD with all thine heart; and lean not unto thine own understanding. In all thy ways acknowledge him, and he shall direct thy paths.*

*D*ay by day, year by year, we re-assess our lives and re-evaluate our plans. Often times we do this without praying first, hearing from God, or allowing Him to order our steps. When we lean to our own thoughts, our past experiences, or even our emotions, we tend to make blunders, and we end up looking around wondering what went wrong. Psalm 37:23 says, *"The steps of a good man are ordered by the Lord."* When we allow God to order our steps by directing our paths, we will walk in victory. Remember, we are victorious in Christ Jesus. We are more than conquerors.

Day 27

Believers have security in God through His name as a strong tower to those who know how to make use of it as such.

> **Proverbs 18:10 NASB**
>
> *The name of the LORD is a strong tower; the righteous runs into it and is safe.*

The righteous, by faith, prayer, devotion towards God, and dependence on Him, run into it, as their city of refuge. Having made sure their interest in God's name, they take the comfort and benefit of it; they go out of themselves, retire from the world, live above, dwell in God and God in them, and so they are safe. They think themselves so, and they shall find themselves so (Matthew Henry Commentary).

Day 28

Isaiah 41:10 NIV

So do not fear, for I am with you; do not be dismayed, for I am your God. I will strengthen you and help you; I will uphold you with my righteous right hand.

*I*n the midst of trials, do not fear. God is with you. He knows your every trial and your every weakness. He is your strength. Lean on His everlasting arms. Allow Him to undergird you. He will hold you up in times of weakness. Fear not, dear heart.

Day 29

*A*s part of the process of Jesus' departure from this earthly realm, He often encouraged His disciples. In this verse, Jesus assures the disciples all will be well with them because He was leaving His peace with them.

> **John 14:27 KJV**
>
> *Peace I leave with you, my peace I give unto you: not as the world giveth, give I unto you. Let not your heart be troubled, neither let it be afraid.*

*W*hen we have the peace of God, we are able to weather the storms of life. With God's peace, our mindset is different. We tend to view things differently. Circumstances that would have once rocked our worlds and caused us to be unsettled will no longer bother us. Peace is a gift that no amount of money can buy. It is a free gift from God that will rid us from fear.

Day 30

> **John 16:33 KJV**
>
> *These things I have spoken unto you, that in me ye might have peace. In the world ye shall have tribulation: but be of good cheer; I have overcome the world.*

We are comforted with the promise of peace in Him, by virtue of His victory over the world. Whatever troubles we might meet within the world, we will yet have the peace of God. These things He has spoken, that in Him we might have peace; and if you do not have it not in Him, we will not have it at all, for in the world we will suffer tribulation. And, although we can expect troubles, we yet may be cheerful, for Jesus has overcome the world.

Day 31

God is our refuge to whom we may flee, and in whom we may be safe and think ourselves so, being secure upon good grounds. God is our strength, to bear us up under our burdens, to fit us for all our services and sufferings. He will by His grace put strength into us, and on Him, we may stay ourselves. It is our duty, it is our privilege, to be thus fearless; it is an evidence of a clear conscience, of an honest heart, and of a lively faith in God and His providence and promise.

> **Psalm 46:1-3 KJV**
>
> *God is our refuge and strength, a very present help in trouble. Therefore will not we fear, though the earth be removed, and though the mountains be carried into the midst of the sea;* **Though** *the waters thereof roar and be troubled,* **though** *the mountains shake with the swelling thereof. Selah.*

Day 32

> **Psalm 16:8 KJV**
>
> *I have set the LORD always before me: because **he** is at my right hand, I shall not be moved.*

*I*t is with wisdom and duty to set the Lord always before us, and to see Him continually at our right hand, wherever we are, to eye Him as our chief good and highest end, our owner, ruler, and judge, our gracious benefactor, our sure guide and strict observer; and, while we do this, we shall not be moved either from our duty or from our comfort. Blessed Paul set the Lord before him, when, though bonds and afflictions did await him, he could bravely say, "None of these things move me."

*T*hat, if our eyes be ever towards God, our hearts and tongues may ever rejoice in Him; it is our own fault if they do not. If the heart rejoices in God, out of the abundance of that let the mouth speak, to His glory, and the edification of others (Matthew Henry Commentary).

Day 33

*C*are is a burden; it makes the heart stoop; we must cast our cares upon God by faith and prayer, commit our way and works to Him; let Him do as it seems Him good, and we will be satisfied. To cast our burden upon God is to stay

> **Psalm 55:22 NIV**
>
> *Cast your cares on the LORD and he will sustain you; he will never let the righteous be shaken.*

ourselves in His providence and promise, and to be very easy in the assurance that all shall work for good.

*I*f we do so, it is promised, 1. That He will sustain us, both support and supply us, will Himself carry us in the arms of His power, as the nurse carries the sucking-child, will strengthen our spirits so by His Spirit as that they shall sustain the infirmity. He has not promised to free us immediately from that trouble, which gives rise to our cares and fears, but He will provide that we be not tempted above what we are able, and that we shall be able according as we are tempted. 2. That He will never suffer the righteous to be moved, to be so shaken by any troubles as to quit either their duty to God or their comfort in Him. [And], He will not suffer them to be moved forever though they fall, they shall not be utterly cast down (Matthew Henry Commentary).

Day 34

I Peter 5:7 JB2000
Casting all your cares upon him, for he cares for you.

*T*hrow your cares, which are so cutting, distracting, wounding your souls, and piercing your hearts, upon the wise and gracious providence of God. Trust in Him with a firmly composed mind, *for he cares for us*. He is willing to release us of our cares and take them upon Himself. He loves us just that much.

Day 35

The nature of the Word of God, and the great intention of giving it to the world is for it to be a *lamp and a light*. It directs us in our work and

> **Psalm 119:105 KJV**
>
> *Thy word is a lamp unto my feet, and a light unto my path.*

way, and a dark place indeed the world would be without it. It is a lamp which we may set up by us and take into our hands for our own particular use (Prov. 6:23). The commandment is a lamp kept burning with the oil of the Spirit; it is like the lamps in the sanctuary and the pillar of fire to Israel. The use is what we make of it. It must be not only a *light to our eyes*, to gratify them, and fill our heads with speculations, but a *light to our feet* and *to our path*, to direct us in the right ordering of our conversation, both in the choice of our way in general and in the particular steps we take in that way, that we may not take a false way nor a false step in the right way. We are then truly sensible of God's goodness to us in giving us such a lamp and light when we make it a guide to our feet, our path.

Day 36

Psalm 118:14-16 KJV

The LORD is my strength and song, and is become my salvation. The voice of rejoicing and salvation is in the tabernacles of the righteous: the right hand of the LORD doeth valiantly. The right hand of the LORD is exalted: the right hand of the LORD doeth valiantly.

The Lord is my strength and my song; that is, I make Him so (without Him, I am weak and sad, but on Him, I stay myself as my strength, both for doing and suffering, and in Him, I solace myself as my song, by which I both express my joy and ease my grief), and, making Him so, I find Him so: He strengthens my heart with His graces and gladdens my heart with His comforts. If God is our strength, He must be our song; if He works all our works in us, He must have all praise and glory from us. God is sometimes the strength of His people when He is not their song; they have spiritual supports when they want spiritual delights. But, if He is both to us, we have abundant reason to triumph in Him; for, He is our strength and our song, He has become not only our Savior, but our salvation; for His being our strength is our protection to the salvation, and His being our song is an earnest and foretaste of the salvation (Matthew Henry Commentary).

Day 37

*I*n an effort to live holy, by the statutes of God, we must watch the company we keep. Yes, those who engage in evil (ungodly acts) will always be in our midst. However, just because we live in a society

> **Psalm 119:114-115 NIV**
>
> *You are my refuge and my shield; I have put my hope in your word. Away from me, you evildoers, that I may keep the commands of my God!*

amongst them does not mean we should engage regularly with them. One of two things will happen when engaging regularly with those who are not equally yoked spiritually. One, we will succumb to their lifestyle. Or, two, they will succumb to ours.

*I*s having your faith weakened a chance you want to take? Do you want to be overcome with evil? Or, has your faith been fortified enough to overcome evil with good?

Day 38

Psalm 119:25 NIV

I am laid low in the dust; preserve my life according to your word.

*N*o matter how low life takes us, our lives can be preserved by the Lord our God, through His Word. His Word is our saving grace. It breeds life, hope, faithfulness, fulfillment, desire, promise, blessings, truth, joy, love, righteousness, patience, meekness, faith, gentleness and self-control.

Day 39

God's promises are found in His Word. We have a promise in Hebrews 13:5, where God tells us He will never leave us nor forsake us. In Luke 20:43, He promises He will make our enemies our footstool. Daniel 12:2 promises us everlasting life after an earthly death. In the abundance of His Word are an abundance of promises. There, we shall find comfort.

> **Psalm 119: 50 NIV**
>
> *My comfort in my suffering is this: Your promise preserves my life.*

Day 40

Psalm 119:71 NIV

It was good for me to be afflicted so that I might learn your decrees.

*W*hen believers are afflicted, they desperately search the scriptures for God's words that are applicable to their situation. Without the afflictions, would you truly search through and learn God's decrees?

Afflictions and troubling times tend to draw us closer to God. We tend to pray more, study more and commune more with our Heavenly Father. Sometimes, trials come to get our attention. But, it is not for us to focus on the trial, but to focus on Him who is able to deliver us safely out of it.

Day 41

*G*od never turns a deaf ear to His children. He knows all, sees all, and hears all. When we cry out to Him, He hears us and he answers. Praise the Lord, our God!

> **Psalm 120:1 KJV**
>
> *In my distress I cried unto the LORD, and he heard me.*

Day 42

John 14:1-3 KJV

Let not your heart be troubled: ye believe in God, believe also in me. In my Father's house are many mansions: if it were not so, I would have told you. I go to prepare a place for you. And if I go and prepare a place for you, I will come again, and receive you unto myself; that where I am, there ye may be also.

*I*n this passage, Jesus is yet preparing the disciples for His departure from earth. This conversation is pre-crucifixion. He understands His closest friends will certainly miss Him after His earthly ministry is complete and He returns to His heavenly seat. Jesus is attempting to reassure the disciples that it is necessary for Him to leave. If He does not go, He cannot come again to receive us unto Himself.

*W*e often have selfish ways. We think we know what is best for our lives. But, the god we serve is omnipotent. He knows all. If we say we trust Him, we must trust Him implicitly.

Day 43

*I*n this passage, John, the revelator, is sharing the vision God showed him of a time to come. This particular verse describes the time frame of the millennial period, when Christ will reign on earth after the battle of Armageddon where Satan will again be defeated. During the millennial period, Satan will be bound

> **Revelation 21:4 KJV**
>
> *And God shall wipe away all tears from their eyes; and there shall be no more death, neither sorrow, nor crying, neither shall there be any more pain: for the former things are passed away.*

and a new heaven and earth will have been created. The former things (the earth and heavens that exist now) will have passed away.

Day 44

Psalm 23:4 KJV

Yea, though I walk through the valley of the shadow of death, I will fear no evil: for thou art with me; thy rod and thy staff they comfort me.

*W*e will endure turbulent times in our lives and our bodies may become wracked with trepidation. This is a natural response to troubling times. However, we are reminded in Psalm 23, God, who is ever present, is with us. He has a rod and a staff that will protect us and comfort us. Although we may feel alone, we are not. Remember, we were not given the spirit of fear, but of power, love and a sound mind. No matter the circumstances, cast away fear and utilize the power, love, and sound mind you have been given in Christ.

Day 45

*I*t is natural to take on the concerns of daily life. This includes having thoughts about shelter, food, money, gas for the car, clothing, etc. We always try to ensure that each of our needs is met. Is it wrong to have these concerns? Absolutely not! What the Bible is warning us against in

Matthew 6:25 NIV

Therefore I tell you, do not worry about your life, what you will eat or drink; or about your body, what you will wear. Is not life more than food, and the body more than clothes?

Matthew 6:25 is being <u>consumed</u> with worry. There is a difference between being concerned about something and worrying about it. Being concerned means paying the appropriate attention to it to ensure the task is completed. Worrying, on the other hand, is being fixated on a task and letting everything else fall by the wayside. When we worry, we do more harm than good because other important areas of our lives falter because we do not pay them the necessary attention.

*A*dditionally, worry shows our lack of faith in God. Matthew 6 goes on to tell us how God takes care of the birds and then asks us are we not more valuable than they in the eyesight of our creator. It is important that we know who we are to God and understand that He will see that each and every need we have is met.

Day 46

> ### Mark 5:2-8 NIV
>
> *When Jesus got out of the boat, a man with an impure spirit came from the tombs to meet him. This man lived in the tombs, and no one could bind him anymore, not even with a chain. For he had often been chained hand and foot, but he tore the chains apart and broke the irons on his feet. No one was strong enough to subdue him. Night and day among the tombs and in the hills he would cry out and cut himself with stones. When he saw Jesus from a distance, he ran and fell on his knees in front of him. He shouted at the top of his voice, "What do you want with me, Jesus, Son of the Most High God? In God's name don't torture me!" For Jesus had said to him, "Come out of this man, you impure spirit!"*

This is the account of a man who was bound by a legion of spirits. In the midst of his possession, he yet called out to Jesus for deliverance. He knew where he could get his deliverance. He went to the Deliverer. When you find yourself bound by drug abuse, illicit sexual desires, or any other unpleasing habit, God can yet deliver you. He wants you to call on Him. He is able to heal and deliver you by the power that is vested in Him.

Day 47

Romans 12:1-2 is loaded with instructions for believers. First, verse one instructs us to present our bodies unto the Lord. When we present our bodies, we must present them in the proper manner: as a living sacrifice, holy and acceptable unto God. This is our reasonable service.

Reasonable service is the bare minimum. This is the least we can do. Our body is the temple of God, and it must be pure at all times in order for the Spirit to dwell there. Verse 2 instructs us

> **Romans 12:1-2 KJV**
>
> *I beseech you therefore, brethren, by the mercies of God, that ye present your bodies a living sacrifice, holy, acceptable unto God, which is your reasonable service. And be not conformed to this world: but be ye transformed by the renewing of your mind, that ye may prove what is that good, and acceptable, and perfect, will of God.*

and warns us to refrain from conforming to this world system. Instead, we are to transform our minds by the Word of God from our ungodly ways of thinking. Doing so will allow us to prove what is that good, acceptable and perfect will of God.

Day 48

Psalm 32:8-10 ESV

I will instruct you and teach you in the way you should go; I will counsel you with my eye upon you. Be not like a horse or a mule, without understanding, which must be curbed with bit and bridle, or it will not stay near you. Many are the sorrows of the wicked, but steadfast love surrounds the one who trusts in the Lord.

God will not let us go astray or take His eyes off us. He said He will never leave us or forsake us. He will instruct us and teach us about the way we should go, for He is our guide. We are warned not to be stubborn or unwise as animals, but to trust in the Lord whose steadfast love surrounds us.

Day 49

*I*t is commonplace in our modern society to be locked into time schedules and faced with meeting deadlines. With these obligations, we have a tendency to become anxious.

However, we are advised in Phil. 4:4-7, it is better to do all things in moderation and with prayer and supplication. When life becomes overwhelming, we are to go to God and make our requests known. He will give us the peace we need as we endure the trials of life. This peace we will not be able to understand; however, it will keep our hearts and minds through Jesus Christ.

Philippians 4:4-7 KJV

Rejoice in the Lord alway: and again I say, Rejoice. Let your moderation be known unto all men. The Lord is at hand. Be careful for nothing; but in every thing by prayer and supplication with thanksgiving let your requests be made known unto God. And the peace of God, which passeth all understanding, shall keep your hearts and minds through Christ Jesus.

Day 50

II Corin. 12:9-10 KJV

And he said unto me, My grace is sufficient for thee: for my strength is made perfect in weakness. Most gladly therefore will I rather glory in my infirmities, that the power of Christ may rest upon me. Therefore I take pleasure in infirmities, in reproaches, in necessities, in persecutions, in distresses for Christ's sake: for when I am weak, then am I strong.

Jesus was persecuted for spreading the gospel of the good news. As believers, we know that we will suffer persecution for the sake of the gospel also. Even in our persecution, God will not forsake us. In this, we can find solace.

The stress of life can weaken our endurance, but in Christ, we are strengthened. Thus, we are fortified to endure personal attacks, envy, character assassinations, distresses, backbiting, slander, reproach, jealousy, strife, etc. Although attacks of this nature can be emotionally devastating, God's grace is sufficient for us to endure all.

Day 51

*T*he scene portrayed here with Jesus and His disciples out on the sea closes with a question. The question clearly demonstrates the disciples do not have a full understanding of who the man is they call Master. Although they have walked with Him, eaten with Him, and traveled and ministered with Him, they do not yet fully know the power embedded within Him. Do you truly know the man you serve? Do the daily trials you face yet shake you? Is your faith yet to be fortified? Or, do you place your faith in Him and trust Him to deliver you safely through each storm?

> ### Mark 4:37-41 KJV
>
> *And there arose a great storm of wind, and the waves beat into the ship, so that it was now full. And he was in the hinder part of the ship, asleep on a pillow: and they awake him, and say unto him, Master, carest thou not that we perish? And he arose, and rebuked the wind, and said unto the sea, Peace, be still. And the wind ceased, and there was a great calm. And he said unto them, Why are ye so fearful? how is it that ye have no faith? And they feared exceedingly, and said one to another, What manner of man is this, that even the wind and the sea obey him?*

Day 52

> ### Psalm 103:1-4 KJV
>
> *Bless the LORD, O my soul: and all that is within me, bless his holy name. Bless the LORD, O my soul, and forget not all his benefits: Who forgiveth all thine iniquities; who healeth all thy diseases; Who redeemeth thy life from destruction; who crowneth thee with lovingkindness and tender mercies.*

We have many reasons to bless the name of the Lord. He is truly a gracious, loving and merciful god. He does so much more for us than we can even think to ask. Let us not walk in foolishness and forget His blessings, His mercy, His healing virtue, His loving kindness, His saving grace, His divine protection from dangers seen and unseen, and His redemptive blood that was shed on Calvary's cross. He is the Lord our God, and He is due all praise, honor, and glory.

Day 53

*S*alvation from eternal hellfire is a free gift. This simply means you are not required to purchase it nor can you work for it in an attempt to earn it. As Romans 10:9-11 says, if you say with your mouth Jesus is Lord *and* believe in your heart God raised Him from the dead, you *will* be saved. It is truly that simple!

> **Romans 10:9-11 NIV**
>
> *If you declare with your mouth, "Jesus is Lord," and believe in your heart that God raised him from the dead, you will be saved. For it is with your heart that you believe and are justified, and it is with your mouth that you profess your faith and are saved. As Scripture says, "Anyone who believes in him will never be put to shame."*

*H*ave you received the free gift of salvation? If not, you can receive it right now by following the steps in Romans 10:9-11.

Day 54

> **Ephesians 2:4-9 NIV**
>
> *But because of his great love for us, God, who is rich in mercy, made us alive with Christ even when we were dead in transgressions—it is by grace you have been saved. And God raised us up with Christ and seated us with him in the heavenly realms in Christ Jesus, in order that in the coming ages he might show the incomparable riches of his grace, expressed in his kindness to us in Christ Jesus. For it is by grace you have been saved, through faith—and this is not from yourselves, it is the gift of God— not by works, so that no one can boast.*

God is so gracious that He gave us the free gift of salvation. He so loved us that He gave us His only begotten son, and through Him, we can be saved. There is no way to the Father, except through the Son. Again, we can't buy this gift nor is it of ourselves.

Therefore, we cannot boast and take credit for something we have not done.

Salvation is a gift of the Father, manifested through His son Jesus Christ.

Day 55

*W*hen we come into the knowledge and understanding of the depths of Christ's suffering on the cross and what His death means for us, we will desire to walk upright before God.

When we understand Jesus allowed His blood to be shed so our sins could be revealed, we will respond differently to the free gift of salvation. Just because we were born in sin does not mean we should continue to reside there. The shackles and the bands have been loosed.

> **Titus 2:11-14 NIV**
>
> *For the grace of God has appeared that offers salvation to all people. It teaches us to say "No" to ungodliness and worldly passions, and to live self-controlled, upright and godly lives in this present age, while we wait for the blessed hope—the appearing of the glory of our great God and Savior, Jesus Christ, who gave himself for us to redeem us from all wickedness and to purify for himself a people that are his very own, eager to do what is good.*

Day 56

> **John 14:12-14 KJV**
>
> *Verily, verily, I say unto you, He that believeth on me, the works that I do shall he do also; and greater works than these shall he do; because I go unto my Father. And whatsoever ye shall ask in my name, that will I do, that the Father may be glorified in the Son. If ye shall ask any thing in my name, I will do **it.***

*J*esus did great and marvelous works during His time on earth. However, it was imperative that He depart this earth and return to His heavenly seat. And when He departed, He said we will do what He did and more, but in order for these works to be done, one key must exist: we must believe in the Lord Jesus Christ. Additionally, there are greater benefits to believing and doing the works of the Lord. We will then be able to ask anything in His name, and He will answer our request to glorify the Father.

Day 57

*I*t is not uncommon for us to worry. We worry over family members, particularly our children. We worry when there is a downturn in the economy.

> **I Thessalonians 5:16-18 ESV**
>
> *Rejoice always, pray without ceasing, give thanks in all circumstances; for this is the will of God in Christ Jesus for you.*

We worry about our safety in public and on the highways. There is much we *could* worry about. At the same time, there is much to rejoice about and to be thankful for. We should rejoice and give thanks each and every morning when we breathe air into our lungs, when we reach out and hug our loved ones, when we have a job to go to, when we have food and shelter, when we have clothes and shoes to put on, when we have the faculties of our mind, when we have limbs that function properly, and most important when we have another opportunity to praise God. Remember, our focus should be on the goodness of the Lord.

Day 58

*L*et each person honestly examine his/her heart to see what is embedded within. If we claim to have wisdom, what is its source? Is it heavenly wisdom or is it earthly wisdom? Does it drive us to do good and honor the Lord, or does it drive us to wicked-ness and activities that render self-gain? Each day, we should examine ourselves to be sure we are in right standing with God and to be sure our motives are pure.

> ### James 3:13-18 NIV
>
> *Who is wise and understanding among you? Let them show it by their good life, by deeds done in the humility that comes from wisdom. But if you harbor bitter envy and selfish ambition in your hearts, do not boast about it or deny the truth. Such "wisdom" does not come down from heaven but is earthly, unspiritual, demonic. For where you have envy and selfish ambition, there you find disorder and every evil practice. But the wisdom that comes from heaven is first of all pure; then peace-loving, considerate, submissive, full of mercy and good fruit, impartial and sincere. Peacemakers who sow in peace reap a harvest of righteousness.*

Day 59

Hebrews 4:14-16 KJV

Seeing then that we have a great high priest, that is passed into the heavens, Jesus the Son of God, let us hold fast our profession. For we have not an high priest which cannot be touched with the feeling of our infirmities; but was in all points tempted like as we are, yet without sin. Let us therefore come boldly unto the throne of grace, that we may obtain mercy, and find grace to help in time of need.

Striving to live daily without sin is an enormous task. The great thing is, we do not need to conquer our difficulties alone. Jesus, our great high priest, knows exactly what we are going through. He too, during His time on earth, was tempted. Yet, He did not sin. We too can walk in purity through God's grace. Our high priest sits in heaven on the right-hand side of the Father. We have direct access to the throne of grace. Won't you go to Him today, He who is able to comfort, strengthen, and guide you?

Day 60

If we, as believers, heed the instructions of our Lord and walk in the light as He is in the light, we will not stumble; and, for those who thus walk, the Lord indeed can and does guard us from stumbling.

We are presented as faultless because the righteousness of Christ has been imputed unto the believer.

> **Jude 1:24-25 KJV**
>
> *Now unto him that is able to keep you from falling, and to present you faultless before the presence of his glory with exceeding joy, To the only wise God our Saviour, be glory and majesty, dominion and power, both now and ever.*

Day 61

Psalm 73:26 ESV

My flesh and my heart may fail, but God is the strength of my heart and my portion forever.

*B*ut God is the strength of our hearts and our portion forever. Our God would not fail us, either as protection or a joy. Our hearts would be kept up by divine love and filled eternally with divine glory. We will do well to follow Asaph's example of casting his anchor. We should cast our anchors in Christ and forever find ourselves bound unto Him. There is nothing desirable except God; let us, then, desire only Him. All other things must pass away; let our hearts abide in Him, who alone abides forever.

Day 62

*W*e may be doing what God has called us to do, following Him, and moving toward heaven, and yet be troubled on every side. We may cry out to the Lord, as our fear leads us to pray, and that is great. God brings us into troubles, so He may bring us to our knees. It is always our duty and in our best interest, when we cannot get out of

> **Exodus 14:13-14 NIV**
>
> *But Moses told the people, "Don't be afraid. Just stand still and watch the Lord rescue you today. The Egyptians you see today will never be seen again. The Lord himself will fight for you. Just stay calm."*

troubles and to conquer our fears, to pray and not silence our faith and hope. We must await God's orders and observe them. We must compose ourselves, by confidence in God, into peaceful thoughts of the great salvation God is about to work for us. If God brings us into troubles, He will surely provide a way to bring us out.

Day 63

> **Psalm 23:1 KJV**
> *The LORD **is** my shepherd; I shall not want.*

This verse demonstrates the great care that God takes of believers. He is our shepherd, and we may call Him so. The great confidence we have in God is this: If the Lord is my shepherd, my feeder, I may conclude I shall not want anything that is really necessary and good for me. I shall be supplied with whatever I need, and if I have not everything I desire, I may conclude it is either not fit for me or not good for me or I shall have it in due time.

Day 64

There are at least three interpretations for this verse, and all are applicable to the King of glory. First, it refers to the ascension of Christ into heaven, and the welcome given to Him

> **Psalm 24:7 KJV**
>
> *Lift up your heads, O ye gates; and be ye lift up, ye everlasting doors; and the King of glory shall come in.*

there. Our Redeemer found the gates of heaven shut, but having by His blood made atonement for sin, as one having authority, He demanded entrance. Second, it can refer to Christ's entrance into the souls of men by His Word and Spirit, that they may be His temples. Behold, He stands at the door, and knocks (Revelation 3:20). The gates and doors of the heart are to be opened to Him, as possession is delivered to the rightful owner. Third, it also may refer to His second coming with glorious power. Lord, open the everlasting door of our souls by thy grace, that we may now receive thee, and be completely yours, and that, at length, we may be numbered with your saints in glory.

Day 65

> **Proverbs 17:22 KJV**
>
> *A merry heart doeth good like a medicine: but a broken spirit drieth the bones.*

Stress, anxiety, and depression are death to our bodies. They kill us from the inside out. They are like a poison seeping from one part of us to another, like a cancer. However, when we are filled with joy, our heart is fulfilled. Joy, as an emotion, has the same power as debilitating emotions, but it has the opposite effect. Joy is like a medicine that cures us. It causes life to grow within us and purifies our innermost parts.

Day 66

*E*veryone has an opinion about almost everything. And their opinions usually lead to advice for others. However, the question we need to ask ourselves is: What is the basis or the foundation for their opinion/ advice? Is their advice based on their personal experiences? Experience is a life teacher, but not everyone's experience is the

> **Psalm 1:1 KJV**
>
> *Blessed is the man that walketh not in the counsel of the ungodly, nor standeth in the way of sinners, nor sitteth in the seat of the scornful.*

same. Therefore, we can share our testimonies/ experiences, but they do not dictate what will necessarily happen to others. Are the opinions based on sinful practices? It is imperative that believers are careful who they receive advise from. Living by the Word of God means not only using the statutes that come directly from His Word, but also counsel that comes from others that aligns with His Word.

Day 67

When we are filled with joy, we have a tendency to speak positive words, words of life and encouragement about our own situation, about others, and unto others. In contrast, when our hearts are filled with sorrow or regret, we have a tendency to speak from our brokenness. These words spew venom and poison those around us and even cause greater damage to ourselves. To overcome a broken spirit, strengthen your relationship with Christ, delve into His Word, and fortify your faith in Him by continually hearing His Word. Remember, we are more than conquerors in Christ Jesus!

> **Proverbs 15:13-15 KJV**
>
> *A merry heart maketh a cheerful countenance: but by sorrow of the heart the spirit is broken. The heart of him that hath understanding seeketh knowledge: but the mouth of fools feedeth on foolishness. All the days of the afflicted are evil: but he that is of a merry heart hath a continual feast.*

Day 68

*T*his portion of scripture references Jesus' crucifixion. He was placed between two thieves and a conversation ensued. At the end of the conversation, one thief spoke up and requested, "Remember me when you come into your

> **Luke 23:32 NASB**
>
> *But I have prayed for you, that your faith may not fail; and you, when once you have turned again, strengthen your brothers.*

kingdom." And Jesus replied, "Today, you shall be with me in paradise." This conversation should serve as an example to us. Regardless of whatever trial we may face, we are to find ourselves full of the faith we have in Christ Jesus. The thief whose very life was about to be taken yet believed that Jesus was the Son of God. His faith ushered him into the heavenly kingdom.

*A*dditionally, the last portion of the verse encourages us to strengthen our brothers. Some say, "I am working out my own soul salvation." This is to say they are concerned about themselves only. However, we are reminded to care for one another and to love our neighbor as ourselves. Therefore, as we strengthen and fortify our own faith, we should help others to do the same, so their faith will not fail them.

Day 69

> **Hebrews 11:6 KJV**
>
> *But without faith it is impossible to please him: for he that cometh to God must believe that he is, and that he is a rewarder of them that diligently seek him.*

*I*t has been said by many that it is virtually impossible to keep all of God's commandments. The same faith that enabled us to believe in God and come to Him is the same faith that will allow us to walk in His way and please Him. Therefore, if we want to please God by honoring His Word, we must build our faith, because without faith it is impossible to please God. So, how do we build our faith? Faith cometh by hearing, and by hearing the Word of God (Romans 10:17).

Day 70

*I*n order to operate effect-tively in the earth realm, it is imperative that we have keys for the kingdom of heaven. Jesus has given us words of wisdom that well equip us to operate effect-tively while here on earth. In this passage, He tells us He will honor in heaven our words that we speak here on earth.

> **Matthew 16:19 NIV**
>
> *I will give you the keys of the kingdom of heaven; whatever you bind on earth will be bound in heaven, and whatever you loose on earth will be loosed in heaven.*

Day 71

> **Luke 22:31-32 KJV**
>
> *And the Lord said, Simon, Simon, behold, Satan hath desired to have you, that he may sift you as wheat: But I have prayed for thee, that thy faith fail not: and when thou art converted, strengthen thy brethren.*

God said in His Word what He has for us is good and not evil. God wants only the best for us. It is His desire that we do not fail in our faith, and as we are strengthened, we will strengthen our brother. On the other hand, Satan wants us to be completely destroyed, demolished, and turned asunder. The Bible says we are not ignorant of Satan devices. Just because we know what they are does not mean he is not willing to use them against us. In order for us to not fall victim to the enemy, we must strengthen our faith and strengthen our brother as well.

Day 72

God has supplied for us everything that pertains to life and godliness. It is He who has given us knowledge and wisdom. He even inserted a clause that says if anyone lacks wisdom let him ask. Therefore, we are without excuse. But when we reject the knowledge of God, imminent destruction is on the horizon.

> **Hosea 4:6 KJV**
>
> *My people are destroyed for lack of knowledge: because thou hast rejected knowledge, I will also reject thee, that thou shalt be no priest to me: seeing thou hast forgotten the law of thy God, I will also forget thy children.*

Day 73

Hebrews 10:38 KJV

Now the just shall live by faith: but if any man draw back, my soul shall have no pleasure in him.

Now the just, the justified person, shall live in God's favor a spiritual and holy life, by faith, as long as he retains that gift of God. But if he draws back, if he makes a shipwreck of his faith, God's soul has no pleasure in him. That is, He abhors him and casts him off (Habakkuk 2:3).

Day 74

*L*ife and death are in the power of our tongue. What we speak is what we shall have. If we speak death and negativity into our situation and into our life, that

> **Proverbs 18:21 KJV**
>
> *Death and life are in the power of the tongue: and they that love it shall eat the fruit thereof.*

is what we shall have. Likewise, if we speak positive words, they will manifest in our lives.

Day 75

The truths of God are as pointers/directives to those who

Ecclesiastes 12:11 KJV

The words of the wise are as goads, and as nails fastened by the masters of assemblies, which are given from one shepherd.

are dull and draw back, and nails to those who wander and draw aside. Wise words establish the heart, so we may never sit loose in our duties, nor be taken from them. The Shepherd of Israel is the giver of inspired wisdom. Teachers and guides all receive their communications from Him (Adapted from Matthew Henry Commentary).

Day 76

Jesus was the only human who was without sin. He who knew no sin took upon Himself the sins of the world. His action was for the purpose of delivering unto us salvation, redemption, and forgiveness. Because of His wounds, His bruises, His chastisement, and His stripes, our transgressions are forgiven; our hidden and unconfessed sins are washed away; we have

> **Isaiah 53:5 KJV**
>
> *But he was wounded for our transgressions, he was bruised for our iniquities: the chastisement of our peace was upon him; and with his stripes we are healed.*

peace; and we have divine healing available to us. What greater gift can sinful people ask for than for someone else to bear the burdens of their actions and their wrongdoings? God loved us that much that He gave His only begotten son, and Christ loved us that much that He willingly laid His life down for us!

Day 77

> **Exodus 15:26 ESV**
>
> *"If you will diligently listen to the voice of the LORD your God, and do that which is right in his eyes, and give ear to his commandments and keep all his statutes, I will put none of the diseases on you that I put on the Egyptians, for I am the LORD, your healer."*

But in every trial, we should cast our care upon the Lord, and pour out our hearts before Him. We shall then find that a submissive will, a peaceful conscience, and the comforts of the Holy Ghost, will render the bitterest trial tolerable, yea, pleasant. Moses did what the people had neglected to do; he cried unto the Lord.

And God provided graciously for them. He directed Moses to a tree which he cast into the waters, when, at once, they were made sweet. Some make this tree typical of the cross of Christ, which sweetens the bitter waters of affliction to all the faithful, and enables them to rejoice in tribulation. But a rebellious Israelite shall fare no better than a rebellious Egyptian. The threatening is implied only; the promise is expressed. God is the great physician. If we are kept well, it is He that keeps us; if we are made well, it is He that recovers us. He is our life and the length of our days. Let us not forget that we are kept from destruction and delivered from our enemies, to be the Lord's servants.

Day 78

*F*aith always has been the mark of God's servants, from the beginning of the world. Where the principle is planted by the regenerating Spirit of God, it will cause the truth to be received, concerning justification by the sufferings and merits of Christ. And the same things that are the object of our hope are the objects of our faith. It is a firm persuasion and expectation that God will perform all He has promised to us in Christ. This persuasion allows the soul to enjoy those things now; it gives them a subsistence or reality in the soul, by the first-fruits and foretastes of them. Faith affirms to the mind, the reality of things that cannot be seen by the natural eye. It is a full approval of all God has revealed, as holy, just, and good.

> **Hebrews 11:1-3 KJV**
>
> *Now faith is the substance of things hoped for, the evidence of things not seen. For by it the elders obtained a good report. Through faith we understand that the worlds were framed by the word of God, so that things which are seen were not made of things which do appear.*

Day 79

Hebrews 10:35 KJV

Cast not away therefore your confidence, which hath great recompence of reward.

When you lack confidence in any particular thing, you fail to stay involved in it. When you fail to stay involved, you will not reap the benefits of your activity. For example, if you fail to see your current job as a stepping-stone and decide to not give it your all or even to walk away from it, you will not reap the benefits of that particular job. The benefits could include pay, recommendations for future jobs, promotion, and extended experience and knowledge. It is the same way with God. If you cast away the confidence you have in Him and His Word, you will not reap the benefits that lie within, such as eternal life, everlasting peace, forgiveness, riches, etc.

Day 80

*T*he Bible warns us about being like children, tossed to and fro, and carried about with every wind of doctrine (Eph. 4:14). This causes instability. In an attempt to

> **Hebrews 13:8 KJV**
> *Jesus Christ the same yesterday, and to day, and for ever.*

gain stability, we find ourselves changing to adapt to one situation after another. It is God's desire that we find ourselves rooted and grounded in His Word. Doing so will enable us to be stable (steadfast and unmovable). Also, we find ourselves able to see God and Christ for who they truly are: the same yesterday, today, and forever. When we are flighty and rocked with instability, we are unable to see the truth for what it is. Become grounded today, and let your roots grow deep, as a tree planted by the rivers of water.

Day 81

Isaiah 55:11 ESV

So shall my word be that goes out from my mouth; it shall not return to me empty, but it shall accomplish that which I purpose, and shall succeed in the thing for which I sent it.

God is not a man that He should lie. He does not issue promises that will go unfulfilled. He does not raise our hopes and then let us down. He does not increase our expectations and then fail to deliver. God is a just and honorable god. We can fully expect that His Word, that goes out of His mouth, will be fulfilled. It will accomplish that for which it was sent.

Day 82

*F*or God (Father, Son, and Spirit) is faithful that promised. God the Father is a promising god and is known to be so by His people; He is eminently and emphatically the Promiser. The promises of

> **Hebrews 10:23 KJV**
>
> *Let us hold fast the profession of our faith without wavering; (for he is faithful that promised).*

God are exceeding great and precious, very ancient, free, and unconditional, irrevocable and immutable, and are admirably suited to the cases of His people and will be fulfilled- every one of them. His promises include in them things temporal, spiritual, and eternal. God is faithful to all His promises, nor can He fail or deceive. He is all wise and foreknowing of everything that comes to pass. He never changes His mind nor forgets His Word. He is able to perform His Word. He is the God of truth and cannot lie; nor has He ever failed in anyone of His promises, nor will He suffer His faithfulness to fail; and this is a strong argument to hold fast a profession of faith.

Day 83

Hebrews 6:10 KJV

For God is not unrighteous to forget your work and labour of love, which ye have shewed toward his name, in that ye have ministered to the saints, and do minister.

As we are faithful in ministering to others, as God has called us to do, we can rest assured He, as a righteous god, will not forget the labor of our hands and the love we showed. For our works, we shall receive a crown of glory (I Peter 5:1-4).

Day 84

*M*ankind was made in the image of God and His likeness. Just as man experiences a range of emotions, so does God, the creator. God has a wrath, and His wrath is dispensed upon mankind as He wills. However, God's anger lasts for just a moment. His favor, however, is long lasting and breeds life. Likewise, times of trouble do not last always. At the end of weeping, from the torments of trouble, comes joy!

> **Psalm 30:5 KJV**
>
> *For his anger endureth but a moment; in his favour is life: weeping may endure for a night, but joy cometh in the morning.*

Day 85

> **James 1:2 KJV**
>
> *My brethren, count it all joy when ye fall into divers temptations.*

Many times, we believe because we are faced with trials and challenges that we have a license to have a pity party. As a result, we complain to anyone who has an ear to listen to us. *BUT*, the Word tells us to rejoice always. Regardless of what we find ourselves faced with, we must be joyful and place our troubles in God's capable hands knowing that He will be our guide as we navigate through them.

Day 86

*W*e are warned against complaining and coveting what others have. We are to be content with the things God has blessed us with and with the knowledge of knowing He will never leave or forsake us. In and through it all, we can boldly declare, "The Lord is my helper, and I shall not fear what man shall do unto me," because we know God is on our side.

> **Hebrews 13:5-6 KJV**
>
> *Let your conversation be without covetousness; and be content with such things as ye have: for he hath said, I will never leave thee, nor forsake thee. So that we may boldly say, The Lord is my helper, and I will not fear what man shall do unto me.*

Day 87

Philippians 4:6-7 NIV
Do not be anxious about anything, but in every situation, by prayer and petition, with thanksgiving, present your requests to God. And the peace of God, which transcends all understanding, will guard your hearts and your minds in Christ Jesus.

The world lives by a 'right now' mentality. We want everything quickly, as though we can pop our desires into a microwave and have them return to us instantaneously. We have lost our patience to wait for the appropriate time. However, we are warned in the Word of God to be patient in all things. We must pray while we wait and make our petitions known unto God.

Day 88

Apostle Paul shares words of encouragement to ancient-day believers that is yet applicable to modern-day believers. It is imperative that we know who we are in Christ Jesus. Like Paul, we should be fully persuaded that no matter what force may come against us: death (the crucifixion of Christ), life (with its afflictions/ trials), angels (good or evil), principalities/ powers (not even those with the highest rank),

> **Romans 8:37-39 KJV**
>
> *Nay, in all these things we are more than conquerors through him that loved us. For I am persuaded, that neither death, nor life, nor angels, nor principalities, nor powers, nor things present, nor things to come, Nor height, nor depth, nor any other creature, shall be able to separate us from the love of God, which is in Christ Jesus our Lord.*

not our past nor our future, height nor depth (mountains, barriers, the great abyss), or creatures (nothing beneath the Almighty God), we will not be separated from God's love.

Day 89

> **James 1:5 NASB**
>
> *But if any of you lacks wisdom, let him ask of God, who gives to all generously and without reproach, and it will be given to him.*

*W*e should desire the wisdom of God to conduct our daily affairs: to observe the providences of God, in order to follow them, to make the proper use of them, not to be lifted up too much in prosperity, and to avoid excessive distress in adversity. We need wisdom to operate effectively in matters of the spirit: obtaining more grace (the truest wisdom), a better understanding and knowledge base of the gospel (the hidden wisdom of God), the wisdom to engage with those who are outside the body and to engage with those who are within the body.

*I*f we lack wisdom to operate in everyday life and in spiritual matters, we can ask of God, the giver of all good gifts. Make your request known unto the Lord. Do it today! (Adapted from John Gill's commentary.)

Day 90

Nowhere in the Bible are we told or promised we will not suffer, endure trials, reap persecution, or have troubles as believers. On the converse, we are told we will. Psalm 34:19 begins with a direct, clear

> **Psalm 34:19 ESV**
>
> *Many are the afflictions of the righteous, but the LORD delivers him out of them all.*

statement: *Many are the afflictions of the righteous...* Therefore, we need not to guess or wonder whether or not we will be troubled because we are told we will be. Rather, we should take delight in the latter portion of the verse: ... but the Lord delivers him out of them all. Hooray! Our Savior will come to our rescue!

Day 91

> **II Corin. 4:8-9 KJV**
>
> **We are** troubled on every side, yet not distressed; **we are** perplexed, but not in despair; Persecuted, but not forsaken; cast down, but not destroyed.

We face trouble from every direction but regardless of the trials, our faith will make us strong.

Although we may be faced with a trial, we are not overcome. We are not defeated. We are not destroyed. We are victorious. We are more than conquerors.

Day 92

*D*uring times of calamity, be it a plague, war, pestilence, or famine believers around us will suffer and/or perish. But, we the believers in Christ Jesus will not be touched. Be reminded of the Israelites who were in Egypt during the time God sent ten plagues. The Egyptians fell dead

> **Psalm 91:7 NIV**
>
> *A thousand may fall at your side, ten thousand at your right hand, but it will not come near you.*

all around the Israelites, while the Israelites remained untouched. When the Israelites left Egypt and were followed by Pharaoh's army, they passed safely through the Red Sea. But when the Egyptians attempted to pass through the Red Sea, they were demolished. Trust in the Lord and know your destiny will not be to perish.

Day 93

> **Psalm 23:4-6 KJV**
>
> *Yea, though I walk through the valley of the shadow of death, I will fear no evil: for thou art with me; thy rod and thy staff they comfort me. Thou preparest a table before me in the presence of mine enemies: thou anointest my head with oil; my cup runneth over. Surely goodness and mercy shall follow me all the days of my life: and I will dwell in the house of the LORD for ever.*

The valley of the shadow of death may denote the most severe and terrible affliction. Death is like a valley that we must pass through to go from this life to our eternal life. Yet, it is the shadow of death that we will experience. The shadow of death, like the shadow of a serpent, has no sting, for Jesus has taken the sting out of death (I Cor. 15:55).

Valleys also are often fruitful. In passing through death's valley, we get the fruit of everlasting life, if we have received the free gift of salvation. Knowing this, the people of God are comforted. At the Lord's table, believers will partake of a feast. As believers are anointed with the Holy Spirit and drink from the everlasting cup, they are comforted. As we trust that God's goodness and mercy will follow us each and every day, we will seek happiness here on earth as we serve God. Then, we shall rejoice in His love forever in heaven.

Day 94

Christ is a physician; He is Jehovah Rapha, the god that heals. Many are the diseases of His people, and He heals them all by His blood, stripes, and wounds. He heals those with

> **Psalm 147:3 ESV**
>
> *He heals the brokenhearted and binds up their wounds.*

broken hearts, by pouring in oil or by applying pardoning grace and mercy to them, which streams through His blood (Adapted from John Gill's Exposition of the Entire Bible.)

Day 95

Matthew 5:4 NASB
Blessed are those who mourn, for they shall be comforted.

Death is a natural part of life. Hebrews 9:27 says, *"And as it is appointed unto men once to die, but after this the judgment."* With death comes mourning. Mourning is a time of sorrow. Although we can rejoice when our loved ones who were believers pass over into glory (to be absent from the body is to be present with the Lord- II Cor. 5:8), we are yet saddened because our time of fellowship with them ceases until a future date. In our time of mourning, the Lord comforts us.

(Note- mourning also occurs with other types of losses, such as income (job), housing (shelter), friendships and possessions. In all losses, as we mourn, we will be comforted.)

Day 96

Because times have changed, customs and practices have been forfeited/disregarded, and familial relations are off kilter, people often think scriptural references are not applicable to the people of today. Although circumstances may not be exactly the same, principles yet remain.

> **Romans 15:4 NIV**
>
> *Such things were written in the Scriptures long ago to teach us. And the Scriptures give us hope and encouragement as we wait patiently for God's promises to be fulfilled.*

The scriptural references of yesterday's situations are for our learning today. When we read of someone suffering through a trial and how they made it through safely by God's grace, we become hopeful, knowing we too can be delivered. God is no respecter of persons. He is the same yesterday, today, and forever. What He did for the saints of old, He will do for the saints of today.

Day 97

Matthew 11:28 ESV

Come to me, all who labor and are heavy laden, and I will give you rest.

*W*hen the cares of the world wear us down, both physically and emotionally, we can find rest in our Creator, for He cares for us. Sinners, wearied in the ways of iniquity, are invited to come to Christ and find speedy relief. Penitents, burdened with the guilt of their crimes, may come to this Sacrifice, and find instant pardon. Believers, sorely tempted, and oppressed by the remains of the carnal mind, may come to this blood that cleanses us from all unrighteousness. Purified from all sin, and powerfully assisted in every temptation, they shall find uninterrupted rest in the complete Savior. All are invited to come, and all are promised rest. If few find rest from sin and vile affections, it is because few come to Christ to receive it.

Day 98

'Blessed be God' is an ascription of praise and glory to God, for He can only be blessed of men, by their praising and glorifying him, or by ascribing honor and

II Corinthians 1:3 KJV

Blessed be God, even the Father of our Lord Jesus Christ, the Father of mercies, and the God of all comfort.

blessings to Him. In this form of blessing, He is described, first by His relation to Christ, even the Father of our Lord Jesus Christ, His only begotten Son, His own proper Son, His natural and eternal Son, is of the same nature with Him and equal to Him in perfections, power, and glory. Next, He is described by His attribute of mercy (the Father of mercies), as He has a merciful disposition to His creation. God is also described by His work of comforting the saints (the God of all comfort). There is no solid comfort but what comes from Him; all spiritual comfort is of Him.

Day 99

Psalm 46:1 KJV

God is our refuge and strength, a very present help in trouble.

This psalm encourages us to hope and trust in God, in His power and providence and His gracious presence. We may apply it to physical and spiritual enemies.

The encouragement we have is that, through Christ, we shall be conquerors over them. He is a Help, a present Help, a Help found, one whom we have found to be so, a Help at hand, one that is always near. We cannot desire a better help, nor shall we ever find the same help in any creature.

Day 100

We are not to be moved by what we can see with our **natural eyes** because those things are temporary. They will not last. Instead, we are to focus on those things that are everlasting. To focus on what is eternal, we must look with our spiritual eyes. That is, we must use our **spiritual discernment**.

> **II Corinthians 4:18**
>
> *While we look not at the things which are seen, but at the things which are not seen: for the things which are seen are temporal; but the things which are not seen are eternal.*

Day 101

> **Romans 8:35 KJV**
>
> *Who shall separate us from the love of Christ? shall tribulation, or distress, or persecution, or famine, or nakedness, or peril, or sword?*

"The love of Christ" does not mean the saints' love to Christ, but His love to them; the apostle is speaking not of our love to Christ, but of the love of God and Christ to us, not tribulation or affliction; or distress (whether of body or mind) or persecution (from the world, for this is rather an evidence that Christ has loved us, chosen and called us, because the world hates us); or famine (want of the necessities of life, as food and drink); or nakedness (desire of adequate clothing) or peril (dangers); or sword (death by the sword or any other weapon) can separate us from His love.

Day 102

*H*umility preserves peace and order in all Christian churches and societies; pride, on the other hand, disturbs them. Where God gives grace to be humble, He will give wisdom, faith, and holiness. To be humble, and subject to our reconciled God, will bring greater comfort to the soul than the gratification of pride and ambition. But it is to

> ### I Peter 5:6-7 KJV
> *Humble yourselves therefore under the mighty hand of God, that he may exalt you in due time: Casting all your care upon him; for he careth for you.*

be in due time; not in our desired time, but God's own wisely appointed time. Does He wait, and will not you? What difficulties will not the firm belief of His wisdom, power, and goodness get over! Then, be humble under His hand. Cast "all you care;" personal cares, family cares, cares for the present, and cares for the future, for yourselves, for others, for the church, on God. These are burdensome, and often very sinful, when they arise from unbelief and distrust, when they torture and distract the mind, unfit us for duties, and hinder our delight in the service of God. The remedy is to cast our care upon God and leave every event to His wise and gracious disposal.

Day 103

> **I John 1:9 KJV**
>
> *If we confess our sins, he is faithful and just to forgive us our sins, and to cleanse us from all unrighteousness.*

*W*e must beware of deceiving ourselves in denying or excusing our sins. The more we see them, the more we shall esteem and value the remedy. If we deny them, the truth is not in us, either the truth that is contrary to such denial (we lie in denying our sin), or the truth of religion, is not in us. The Christian religion is the religion of sinners, of such as have sinned, and in whom sin in some measure still dwells. The Christian life is a life of continued repentance, humiliation for and mortification of sin, of continual faith in, thankfulness for, and love to the Redeemer, and hopeful joyful expectation of a day of glorious redemption, in which the believer shall be fully and finally acquitted, and sin abolished forever. If we say we have not sinned, we make Him a liar, and His Word is not in us (I John 1:10).

Day 104

*G*od can turn foes into friends when He pleases. He that has all hearts in His hand has access to men's spirits and power over them, working insensibly,

> **Proverbs 16:7 ESV**
>
> *When a man's ways please the LORD, he makes even his enemies to be at peace with him.*

but irresistibly upon them, can make *a man's enemies to be at peace with him*, can change their minds, or force them into a feigned submission. He can slay all enemies, and bring those together that were at the greatest distance from each other. He will do it for us when we please Him. If we make it our care to be reconciled to God and to keep ourselves in His love, He will incline those that have been envious towards us, and vexatious to us, to entertain a good opinion of us and to become our friends. God made Esau to be at peace with Jacob, Abimelech with Isaac, and David's enemies to court his favor and desire a league with Israel. The image of God appearing upon the righteous and His particular loving kindness to them, are enough to recommend them to the respect of all, even of those that have been most prejudiced against them.

Day 105

Isaiah 26:3 ESV

You keep him in perfect peace whose mind is stayed on you, because he trusts in you.

*T*his is the matter of a promise (Isa. 26:3): *Thou wilt keep him in peace,* in *perfect peace,* inward peace, outward peace, peace with God, peace of conscience, peace at all times, under all events; this peace shall *he* be put into, and kept in the possession of, *whose mind is stayed upon God, because it trusts in him.* It is the character of every good man that he trusts in God, puts himself under His guidance and government, and depends upon Him that it shall be greatly to his advantage to do so. Those that trust in God must have their minds stayed upon Him, must trust Him at all times, under all events, must firmly and faithfully adhere to Him, with an entire satisfaction in Him; and such as do so God will keep in perpetual peace, and that peace shall keep them. When evil tidings are abroad *those* shall calmly expect the event, and not be disturbed by frightful apprehensions arising from them, whose hearts are *fixed, trusting in the Lord* (Ps. 112:7).

Day 106

Concluding these exhort- tations, Paul calls his readers to a life of obe- dience, the right response to the peace of God. The virtues listed are not exhaustive but repre- sentative, and they come to expression in countless ways. Thinking on such things is not an end in itself, but preparation for purposeful action. The Philippians are to be guided both by Paul's teaching and by his example, especially his love for the Philippians.

> **Philippians 4:8-9 NIV**
>
> *Finally, brothers and sisters, whatever is true, whatever is noble, whatever is right, whatever is pure, whatever is lovely, whatever is admirable— if anything is excellent or praiseworthy—think about such things. Whatever you have learned or received or heard from me, or seen in me—put it into practice. And the God of peace will be with you.*

Day 107

Matthew 19:26 NIV
Jesus looked at them and said, "With man this is impossible, but with God all things are possible."

This is a great truth in general, that God is able to do that which quite exceeds all created power; that nothing is too hard for God. When men are at a loss, God is not, for His power is infinite and irresistible; but this truth is here applied to the salvation of any. *Who can be saved*? say the disciples. None, saith Christ, by any created power. *With men this is impossible*: the wisdom of man would soon be surprised in contriving, and the power of man baffled in effecting, the salvation of a soul. No creature can work the change that is necessary to the salvation of a soul, either in itself or in anyone else. With men, it is impossible that so strong a stream should be turned, so hard a heart softened, so stubborn a will bowed. It is a creation, it is a resurrection, and with men, this is impossible; it can never be done by philosophy, medicine, or politics; but *with God all things are possible*.

Day 108

*E*very one of us has an outward and an inward man: a body and a soul. If the outward man perishes, there is no remedy; it must and will be so; it was made

> **II Corinthians 4:16 NASB**
>
> *Therefore we do not lose heart, but though our outer man is decaying, yet our inner man is being renewed day by day.*

to perish. It is our happiness if the decays of the outward man do contribute to the renewing of the inward man, if afflictions outwardly are gain to us inwardly, if when the body is sick, and weak, and perishing, the soul is vigorous and prosperous. The best of men have need of further renewing of the inward man, even day by day. Where the good work is begun there is more work to be done, for carrying it forward. And as in wicked men things grow every day worse and worse, so in godly men, they grow better and better.

Day 109

I John 3:2 NASB
Beloved, now we are children of God, and it has not appeared as yet what we will be. We know that when He appears, we will be like Him, because we will see Him just as He is.

*W*e have the nature of sons by regeneration: we have the title, and spirit, and right to the inheritance of sons by adoption. The time of the revelation of the sons of God in their proper state and glory is deter-mined; and that is when their elder brother comes to call and collect them all together.

Day 110

*T*his new and blessed state when the former things will be passed away will be free from all trouble and sorrow; for, all the effects of former trouble shall be done away. They have been often before in tears, by reason of sin, of affliction, of the calamities of the church; but now *all tears shall be wiped away*; no signs, no remembrance of

> **Revelation 21:4 KJV**
>
> *And God shall wipe away all tears from their eyes; and there shall be no more death, neither sorrow, nor crying, neither shall there be any more pain: for the former things are passed away.*

former sorrows shall remain, any further than to make their present intense happiness the greater. God Himself, as their tender Father, with His own kind hand, *shall wipe away the tears* of His children; and they would not have been without those tears when God shall come and wipe them away. All the causes of future sorrow shall be forever removed: *There shall be neither death nor pain*; and therefore, *no sorrow nor crying*; these are things incident to that state in which they were before, but now all *former things have passed away*.

Day 111

Nehemiah 8:10 NIV
Do not grieve, for the joy of the LORD is your strength.

*T*ake comfort in knowing that you do not have to be strong in your own human strength. The flesh will always fail. But God is our way maker and our strong tower. He will give us the strength to endure the battle. And, He will give us joy unspeakable.

*E*verything is beautiful in its season. We must not be merry when *God calls to mourning*, so we must not frighten and afflict ourselves when God gives us occasion to rejoice. Even sorrow for sin must not grow so excessive as to hinder our joy in God and our cheerfulness in His service.

Day 112

*E*ach day, we put a lot of emphasis on what we need to do to make it or to get ahead. When a new year begins, we look to see how our lives can be better than last year. The Bible tells us to love others as we love ourselves.

*T*herefore, we are to seek to do for others the things we seek to do for ourselves. We must learn how to break free from existentialist thinking and become our brother's keeper. We should not be so consumed with our own lives that we do not have time to make someone else's life better.

> **Matthew 22:37-40 NIV**
>
> *Jesus replied: "'Love the Lord your God with all your heart and with all your soul and with all your mind.' This is the first and greatest commandment. And the second is like it: 'Love your neighbor as yourself.' All the Law and the Prophets hang on these two commandments."*

Day 113

We live in a tempting world, where we are compassed about with snares. Every place, condition, relation, employment, and enjoyment, abounds with them; yet what comfort we can find from this verse! The trials of common Christians are but common trials that others have. God knows what we can bear, and what we can bear up against, and He will ensure we are not overcome, if we rely upon Him, and resolve to approve ourselves faithful to Him.

> ### I Corinthians 10:13 NIV
>
> *No temptation has seized you except what is common to man. And God is faithful; he will not let you be tempted beyond what you can bear. But when you are tempted, he will also provide a way out so that you can stand up under it.*

When you are tempted to sin, meditate on the Word of God that you have hidden in your heart. Think on those things that are pleasing to God. Every sin begins in the mind before they take root in the heart. So, if we take time to meditate on the Word of God when we find ourselves tempted, we can easy diffuse thoughts that are contrary to God's will.

Day 114

*T*hose who trust to their own sufficiency and are overly confident within themselves will overexert themselves and fail to seek God for His grace. They *shall faint and be weary*, and they *fail* in their services, in their conflicts, and under their burdens. *But those that wait on the Lord*, by faith relying upon Him and commit themselves to

> **Isaiah 40:31 KJV**
>
> *They who wait on the Lord will renew their strength. They will mount up with wings like eagles. They will run and not get weary. They will walk and not faint.*

His guidance, shall find that He will not fail them. They *shall renew their strength and* be anointed, with fresh oil. *They shall mount up with wings like eagles.* They shall walk and not faint; they shall run and not grow tired. Allow the Lord to be your guide. Remember, the steps of a good man are ordered by God (Psalm 37:23).

Day 115

> **James 4:7 KJV**
>
> *Submit yourselves therefore to God. Resist the devil, and he will flee from you.*

*W*e as believers should forsake the friendship of the world and watch against the envy and pride which we see prevailing in natural men. Instead, we should learn to glory in our submission to God. We must submit our undestanding to the truths of God and our will to His will. God will not hurt us by His dominion over us, but will do us good.

*I*f we yield to temptations, the devil will continually follow us, but if we put on the whole armor of God, and stand against him, he will depart from us.

Day 116

*T*he world would have us to operate by its rules and regulations, but those rules do not always line up with the Word of God. When the world system wants us to apply rules that are contrary to God's Word, we need to find the courage to deny the attempts of the world. We must stand on the Word of

> **Romans 12:2 KJV**
>
> *And be not conformed to this world: but be ye transformed by the renewing of your mind, that ye may prove what is that good, and acceptable, and perfect, will of God.*

God, finding ourselves steadfast and unmovable. In Christ, we are new creatures, and old things have passed away.

Day 117

Matthew 6:34 NIV

Therefore do not worry about tomorrow, for tomorrow will worry about itself. Each day has enough trouble of its own.

Day after day, we find ourselves overcome with worry about the days that lie ahead. But the Word of God instructs us to not worry about tomorrow. We must not perplex ourselves inordinately about future events, because every day brings along with it its own burden of cares and grievances, as if we look about us, and suffer not our fears to betray the provisions/ assistance which grace and reason offer, it brings along with it its own strength and supply too. We must believe that God knows our needs and He will fulfill them. If wants and troubles be renewed with the day, there are aids and provisions renewed likewise; *compassions*, that are new every morning (Lam. 3:22, 23).

Day 118

*A*ll who profess the Christian faith, that they are new creatures, not only do they have a new heart and new nature, must make a change in Christ, for we are new

> **II Corinthians 5:17 KJV**
>
> *Therefore if any man be in Christ, he is a new creature: old things are passed away; behold, all things are become new.*

creatures. We can no longer continue to do things the way we used to; old thoughts, old principles, and old practices are passed away. We must learn how to operate in a manner that is consistent with living a Christian life. The renewed person acts from new principles, by new rules, with new ends, and in new company. If we don't know how to do that, all we have to do is study the life of Christ. He is our perfect example.

Day 119

1 Corinthians 6:19 NIV

Do you not know that your body is a temple of the Holy Spirit, who is in you, whom you have received from God? You are not your own.

*W*e that are joined to Christ are one spirit with Him. We are yielded up to Him, consecrated and set apart for His use, and are thereby possessed, occupied, and inhabited, by His Holy Spirit. This is the purpose a temple—a place where God dwells. Once we yield our bodies to Christ, we are not our own. We are yielded up to God, possessed by and for God. Our bodies were made by God, for God, and purchased for Him. Therefore, we must keep our bodies pure from unclean substances. Anything that is contrary to the spirit of God defiles our bodies. The Holy Spirit refuses to reside in an unclean temple.

*P*urify yourself today, and invite the God of heaven to reside within!

Day 120

*W*e are called to this peace, to peace with God as our privilege and peace with our brethren as our

Colossians 3:15 KJV

And let the peace of God rule in your hearts.

duty. Being united in one body, we are called to be at peace one with another, as the members of the natural body; for we are the body of Christ, and members in particular (1 Cor. 12:27). To preserve in us this peaceable disposition, we must be thankful. The work of thanksgiving to God is such a sweet and pleasant work that it will help to make us sweet and pleasant towards all men. Instead of envying one another upon account of any particular favors and excellence, be thankful for His mercies, which are common to all of you. And be careful not to complain. Use your mouth to praise the Lord and to thank Him for His goodness. We often times are quick to complain rather than to give praise and thanks.

Day 121

> **Luke 6:38 KJV**
>
> *Give, and it shall be given unto you; good measure, pressed down, and shaken together, and running over, shall men give into your bosom. For with the same measure that ye mete withal it shall be measured to you again.*

*W*hen the instruction to *give* has been properly responded to, God is obligated to fulfill the second part of the verse. Your action prompts God's reaction. God's reaction is the blessing flow. He would not have you give and not make sure you are a receiver as well. When God is giving back to you, He presses the gift down, so He will have room to add more. While God is giving you a good portion and pressing it down to add more, He also shakes the gift. Shaking permits the uneven pieces the opportunity to fit together better, resulting in less unused spaces in the receptacle. At this point, the receptacle used to house God's blessing is now full. There is no more room for any more to fit. However, God does not cease His giving. He continues to pour out until the gift is running over, thus providing us with more than enough for ourselves as well as enough to give others. The gifts that God blesses us with are not *only* for us. They are meant to be shared.

Day 122

Satan is a subtle enemy, and uses many strategies to deceive us, and we should not be ignorant of his devices.

> **II Corinthians 2:11 KJV**
>
> *Lest Satan should get an advantage of us: for we are not ignorant of his devices.*

He is also a watchful adversary, ready to take all advantages against us, and we should be very cautious lest we give him any occasion so to do. Satan, under pretense of showing a just indignation against sin and keeping up a strict and righteous discipline, destroys souls, ruins churches, and brings religion into contempt. This was one of his devices in former times, that persons who fell into any gross sin after baptism and a profession of religion, were never to be restored and received into the communion of the church again, let their repentance be ever so sincere. This cruel and inexorable spirit, under the show of strict religion and discipline, is what the apostle here would caution against, as one of the wiles of Satan.

Day 123

> **James 1:8 KJV**
>
> *A double minded man is unstable in all his ways.*

*W*e must have singleness of thought when standing on a decision that has been made. When we waiver back and forth between a variety of choices and when we fail to keep our word that has been given, we show ourselves to be unreliable and unsure. Instability is not the way of the Lord. Learn to be steadfast and unwavering in your convictions. God's Word warns us against being as children, tossed to and fro by every wind of doctrine. Become rooted and grounded in His Word.

Day 124

*M*any people are walking around spiritually asleep although their physical eyes are open. The Bible warns us to be aware of what is going on around us: Men should always watch and pray. The devil, our enemy, is here to take us out: He comes to steal, kill, and destroy (John 10:10). He means us harm and

> **I Peter 5:8 KJV**
> *Be sober, be vigilant; because your adversary the devil, as a roaring lion, walketh about, seeking whom he may devour.*

no good. We need to keep both our physical and natural eyes and ears open, so we can be aware of the enemy's tactics that come against us, for we are not ignorant of Satan's devices (II Corinthians 2:11).

Day 125

> **I Samuel 16: 7b NIV**
>
> *The LORD does not look at the things man looks at. Man looks at the outward appearance, but the LORD looks at the heart.*

Oftentimes, we are judged by how we appear to others. It may be our attire, culture, facial expressions, hair style, jobs, socio-economic status, dwelling place, or personality by which we are judged. God, however, looks at the integrity of our hearts. We need to ensure that our hearts are right before God. That means we do not sin against His Word, and if we find ourselves outside of God's will, we repent before God and ask for forgiveness and to be strengthened in our areas of weakness.

Day 126

*H*umans have their own ways of doing things and their own ways of thinking. Oftentimes, we fail to remember that we do not know everything.

*T*herefore, it is important for us to consult the Word of God to learn God's perspective on issues that we are faced with. We are warned in Proverbs to lean not to our own under-standing (Proverbs 3:5-6). We

Isaiah 55: 8-9 KJV

For my thoughts are not your thoughts, neither are your ways my ways, saith the LORD. For as the heavens are higher than the earth, so are my ways higher than your ways, and my thoughts than your thoughts.

must consult God to gain wisdom. James 1:5 says, *"If any of you lack wisdom, let him ask of God, that giveth to all men liberally, and upbraideth not; and it shall be given him."*

Day 127

Joshua 24: 15b NIV

But if serving the LORD seems undesirable to you, then choose for yourselves this day whom you will serve, whether the gods your forefathers served beyond the River, or the gods of the Amorites, in whose land you are living. But as for me and my household, we will serve the LORD.

*D*o you hide the light of the Lord under a bushel, or do you walk in the boldness of Christ and proclaim the gospel to every creature? If you have chosen to serve the Lord, serve Him in spirit and in truth! As you do so, do not neglect to spread the gospel within your own household.

*F*or those who have children, the Bible instructs us to *"train up a child in the way he should go, and when he is old, he will not depart from it"* (Proverbs 22:6). The world has enough closet Christians, but we are called to be ambassadors for Christ. Ambassadors take their rightful position- boldly. Are you an ambassador for Christ?

Day 128

𝒜 throne demonstrates authority and commands awe and reverence. A throne of grace additionally demonstrates great encouragement, even to the chief of sinners. There grace reigns and acts with sovereign freedom, power, and bounty. It is our

> **Hebrews 4:16 KJV**
> *Let us therefore come boldly unto the throne of grace, that we may obtain mercy, and find grace to help in time of need.*

duty, and in our interest, to be often found before this throne of grace, waiting on the Lord. It is good for us to be there, so we may obtain mercy and find grace to help in times of need. Mercy and grace are the things we want: mercy to pardon all our sins and grace to purify our souls. Besides the daily dependence we have upon God to supply our daily requirements, there are some seasons in which we will surely need the mercy and grace of God. We should every day put up a petition for mercy.

Day 129

> **Proverbs 11:14 KJV**
>
> *Where no counsel is, the people fall: but in the multitude of counselors there is safety.*

As we walk through our lives, we should be sure to seek guidance from those who are wise. Many have walked where we are trying to go. They can offer us pearls of wisdom to keep us from making shipwrecks.

Where no counsel is, but everything done rashly, or no prudent consultation for the common good, but only caballing for parties and divided interests, the people fall, crumble into factions, fall to pieces, fall together by the ears, and fall an easy prey to their common enemies. Councils of war are necessary to the operations of war; two eyes see more than one; and mutual advice is in order to mutual assistance. In the multitude of counselors, that see their need one of another, and act in concert and with concern for the public welfare, there is safety. In our private affairs, we shall often find it to our advantage to obtain advice with many. If they agree in their advice, our way will be the clearer. If they differ, we shall hear what is to be said on all sides and be better able to determine.

Day 130

*P*ride will have a fall. Those that are of a haughty spirit, that think of themselves above what is meet and look with contempt

> **Proverbs 16:18 NIV**
>
> *Pride goes before destruction, a haughty spirit before a fall.*

upon others, that with their pride affront God and disquiet others, will be brought down, either by repentance or by ruin. It is the honor of God to humble the proud (Job 40:11, 12). It is the act of justice that those who have lifted up themselves should be laid low. Pharaoh, Sennacherib, and Nebuchadnezzar were instances of this. Men cannot punish pride, but either admire it or fear it. Therefore, God will take the punishing of it into His own hands. He alone will deal with proud men. Proud men are frequently most proud, and insolent, and haughty, just before their destruction. When proud men set God's judgments at defiance and think themselves at the greatest distance from them, it is a sign that they are at the door. Therefore, let us not fear the pride of others, but greatly fear pride in ourselves.

Day 131

Romans 12:3 NIV

For by the grace given me I say to every one of you: Do not think of yourself more highly than you ought, but rather think of yourself with sober judgment, in accordance with the measure of faith God has given you.

*A*postle Paul warns us about walking in the proper perspective about who we are. It is one thing to be proud about who God has made you to be. This is the sense of having a healthy self-esteem and walking in the assurance of Christ. However, being prideful (thinking more of yourself than you should) will only lead to destruction. Likewise, when we walk in self-doubt, we face the same challenge. When we have an improper self-concept, we will undoubtedly end up on the wrong path in life. Apostle Paul tells us, we must know who we are and not think more highly or lower of ourselves than who we are.

Day 132

As believers, we are not to be moved by what we see. Rather, we respond to the Word of God. If

> **II Corinthians 5:7 KJV**
> *For we walk by faith, not by sight.*

God's Word says it, we believe it. We do not rely upon sense realm evidence for proof. *"Now faith is the substance of things hoped for, the evidence of things not seen"* (Hebrews 11:1). We walk by faith, knowing that God's Word will not return unto Him void, for He is not a man that He should lie.

Day 133

Romans 14:16 NIV

Do not allow what you consider good to be spoken of as evil.

Be careful about doing anything that may give occasion to others to speak evil, either of the Christian religion in general, or of your Christian liberty in particular. The gospel is your good; the liberties and franchises, the privileges and immunities, granted by it, are your good; your knowledge and strength of grace to discern and use your liberty in things disputed are your good, a good which the weak brother has not. Now, let not this be evil spoken of. It is true we cannot hinder loose and ungoverned tongues from speaking evil of us and of the best things we have; but we must not (if we can help it) give them any occasion to do it. Let not the reproach arise from any default of ours, meaning do not make yourself despicable. For example, do not use your knowledge and strength in such a manner as to give occasion to people to call it presumption, loose walking, and disobedience to God's law. We must deny ourselves in many cases for the preservation of our credit and reputation, forbearing to do that which we rightly know we may lawfully do, when our doing it may be a prejudice to our good name, especially when it has the appearance of evil.

Day 134

*W*hat good does it do for believers to wear masks and try to fool people about our character and our level of integrity, if we have none?

*M*an is concerned about how we appear, but God is concerned about the integrity of our hearts. Let us not be

> **Matthew 23: 28 NIV**
>
> *In the same way, on the outside you appear to people as righteous but on the inside you are full of hypocrisy and wickedness.*

concerned about our outer appearance more than our inner condition. We can only fool people for so long, and we can never fool God.

Day 135

> **II Cor. 8:12 KJV**
>
> *For if there be first a willing mind, it is accepted according to that a man hath, and not according to that he hath not.*

This willing mind is accepted when accompanied with sincere endeavors. When men purpose that which is good, and endeavor, according to their ability, to perform also, God will accept of what they have, or can do, and not reject them for what they have not, and what is not in their power to do. This is true as to other things besides the work of charity. But let us note here that this scripture will by no means justify those who think good meanings are enough, or that good purposes and the profession of a willing mind are sufficient to save them.

Day 136

The preaching of Christ is the joy of all who wish well to His kingdom among men. Because it is for one's good, we should rejoice when the gospel is preached, though it be done in pretense and not in the right spirit. Apostle Paul was so far from envying those who had liberty to preach the gospel while he was under confinement that he rejoiced in the preaching of it even by those who did it in pretense and not in truth. How much more then should we rejoice in the preaching of the gospel by those who do it in truth, or those who do it with an ulterior motive?

Philippians 1:15-18 NIV

It is true that some preach Christ out of envy and rivalry, but others out of goodwill. The latter do so out of love, knowing that I am put here for the defense of the gospel. The former preach Christ out of selfish ambition, not sincerely, supposing that they can stir up trouble for me while I am in chains. But what does it matter? The important thing is that in every way, whether from false motives or true, Christ is preached. And because of this I rejoice.

Day 137

John 15:4 NASB

Abide in Me, and I in you. As the branch cannot bear fruit of itself unless it abides in the vine, so neither can you unless you abide in Me.

*I*t is of the utmost importance that all Christ's disciples constantly depend upon and commune with Him. We must adhere to Him and His Word, deriving knowledge and wisdom from Him. Those who choose to come to Christ must abide in Him: *"Abide in me*, by faith; *and I in you*, by my Spirit; *abide in me*, and then fear not but I will *abide in you*;" for the communion between Christ and believers never fails on His side. We must abide in Christ's Word by regarding it, for it is as a *light to our feet*.

Day 138

The care of ministers must be to approve themselves unto God, to be accepted of Him, by demonstrating that they are so approved unto God. In order to be approved, there must be constant care: Study to

> **II Timothy 2:15 KJV**
>
> *Study to shew thyself approved unto God, a workman that needeth not to be ashamed, rightly dividing the word of truth.*

show thyself to be a workman that needs not be ashamed. Ministers must be workmen; they have work to do. Workmen that are unskillful, unfaithful, or lazy have need to be ashamed, but those who mind their business and keep to their work are workmen that need not be ashamed. And what is their work? It is *rightly to divide the word of truth.* Not to invent a new gospel, but rightly to divide the gospel that is committed to their trust, to speak terror to those to whom terror belongs, comfort to whom comfort; to give everyone his/her portion in due season.

Day 139

> **Philippians 3:10 ESV**
>
> *That I may know him and the power of his resurrection, and may share his sufferings, becoming like him in his death.*

Knowing Christ as accor-ding to this passage is believing in Him: feeling the transforming effects and virtue of His resurrection and suffering. We conform to His death and understand the power of it when we die to sin, as Christ died for sin. When we are crucified with Christ, the flesh and affections of it are mortified, and the world is crucified to us, and we to the world, by virtue of the cross of Christ. This is our conformity to His death. Likewise, as believers, we will suffer persecution in the world in which we live, as Christ Himself did for our sake.

Day 140

Descended from one and the same common ancestor, in Adam we are all akin, that hereby we might be engaged in mutual affection and assistance, as fellow-creatures and brethren. Have we not all one Father who not only breathed into the first man the breath of life, but still breathes it into every man. He gave us these souls; He formed the spirit of man within Him. He not only gave us our life and breath, when He brought

> **Acts 17:26-28 NIV**
>
> *From one man he made all the nations, that they should inhabit the whole earth; and he marked out their appointed times in history and the boundaries of their lands. God did this so that they would seek him and perhaps reach out for him and find him, though he is not far from any one of us. For in him we live and move and have our being.*

us into being, but He is continually giving them to us; His providence is a continued creation; He holds our souls in life; every moment our breath goes forth, but He graciously gives it us again the next moment; it is not only His air that we breathe in, but it is in His hand that our breath is (Dan. 5:23).

Day 141

Psalm 119:103 KJV

How sweet are thy words unto my taste! yea, sweeter than honey to my mouth!

There is such a thing as a spiritual taste, an inward savor and desire of divine things. It is of our personal experience, as we cannot give to others. According to this scripture, the Word of God has a sweet taste, very sweet, sweeter than any of the gratifications of sense, even sweeter than those that are most delicious. David speaks as if he wanted words to express the satisfaction he took in the discoveries of the divine will and grace; no pleasure was comparable to it.

Day 142

Though Christ Himself was in the greatest struggle and agony, as He hung upon Calvary's cross, He yet had a word of comfort to speak to a poor penitent that committed himself to Christ. The lesson for us is, if we are truly penitent about our sins, we, through Christ, will obtain not

> **Luke 23:42-43 NIV**
>
> *Then he said, "Jesus, remember me when you come into your kingdom. Jesus answered him, "Truly I tell you, today you will be with me in paradise.*

only the pardon of our sins, but a place in the paradise of God (Heb. 9:15). This magnifies the riches of free grace given to us by God.

Day 143

> **Ephesians 2:8-9 NLT**
>
> *For by grace you have been saved through faith; and that not of yourselves, it is the gift of God; Salvation is not a reward for the good things we have done, so none of us can boast about it.*

Our faith, our conversion, and our eternal salvation, are not the mere product of any natural abilities, nor of any merit of our own: *Not of works, lest any man should boast.* These things are not brought to pass by anything done by us, and therefore, all boasting is excluded; he who glories must not glory in himself, but in the Lord. There is no room for any man's boasting of his own abilities and power, or as though he had done anything that might deserve such immense favors from God. God, who is rich in mercy, is the orchestrator of this great and happy change, and His great love is the cause of it. And then, by grace we are saved, and by grace are we saved through faith—it is the gift of God.

Day 144

Every answer to our prayers is evidence that the Lord is on our side. Therefore, we need not fear what man can do to us. We should conscientiously do our duty to all, and trust in Him

> **Psalm 118:6 KJV**
>
> *The LORD is on my side; I will not fear: what can man do unto me?*

alone to accept and bless us. Let us seek to live to declare the works of God and to encourage others to serve Him and trust in Him.

Day 145

Ephesians 6:12 NKJV

For we do not wrestle against flesh and blood, but against principalities, against powers, against the rulers of the darkness of this age, against spiritual hosts of wickedness in the heavenly places.

*W*hen we encounter problems with other persons, from our humanness, we want to fight fire with fire. More appropriately, we want to fight flesh with flesh. If someone hurts us with words, we want to return the favor with words. However, when we begin to understand that it is not truly the person who is attacking us, but a spirit that is operating through the person, we will not retaliate in kind. Instead, we will war according to scripture. Ephesians 6:12 tells us that our fight is not against flesh and blood, but against principalities, powers, rulers of darkness, and spiritual wickedness. Therefore, the battle must continue to be fought in the spirit. It begins in the spirit, and must be fought in the spirit, so it can be conquered in the spirit. The weapons of our warfare are not carnal, but mighty through God for the pulling down of strongholds (II Cor. 10:4).

Day 146

Abraham believed God, and the Lord's righteousness was imputed to him. And, he was called the friend of God (2 Chronicles 20:7). He was loved by God with an ever-lasting love, who showed acts of friendship to him. He was called by God's grace and provided spiritual blessings.

> **James 2:23 NIV**
>
> *And the scripture was fulfilled that says, "Abraham believed God, and it was credited to him as righteousness," and he was called God's friend.*

God increased him with the increase of God, favored him with near communion with him, honored him with high characters, and distinguished him by peculiar marks of His favor, and reckoned his enemies and friends as his own (Genesis 12:8) Abraham, on the other hand, loved God and showed himself friendly to Him. He trusted in God and believed His every word. He readily complied with His will and not only yielded a cheerful obedience to His commands, but enjoined his children after him to observe them. Abraham is a great example of obedience for us.

Day 147

> **I Cor. 16:13 NIV**
>
> *Be on your guard; stand firm in the faith; be courageous; be strong.*

*A*postle Paul advises us as believers to *stand fast in the faith*, to keep our ground, adhere to the revelation of God, and not give it up for the wisdom of the world, nor suffer it to be corrupted by it. We must stand for the faith of the gospel and maintain it, even to death. We are to stand in it, so as to abide in the profession of it and feel and yield to its influence. Christians should be fixed in the faith of the gospel and never desert nor renounce it. It is by this faith alone that we will be able to keep our ground in an hour of temptation; it is by faith that we stand (II Cor. 1:24); it is by this that we must overcome the world. Additionally, we are warned against weak faith and being tossed to and fro with every wind of doctrine. We must know what we believe and stand on it.

Day 148

We are charged to preserve the Word of God, pure and entire. Keeping it pure is to refrain from adding to it. Keeping it entire is to refrain from subtracting from it. In practice, "You shall not add by committing the evil

> **Deuteronomy 4:2 KJV**
>
> *Ye shall not add unto the word which I command you, neither shall ye diminish ought from it, that ye may keep the commandments of the LORD your God which I command you.*

which the law forbids, nor diminish by omitting the good which the law requires." In opinion, "You shall not add your own inventions, as if the divine institutions were defective, nor introduce, much less impose, any rites of religious worship other than what God has appointed; nor shall you diminish, or set aside, anything that is appointed, as needless or superfluous." God's work is perfect; nothing should be added to it, nor taken from it.

Day 149

Lam. 3:32 KJV

But though he cause grief, yet will he have compassion according to the multitude of his mercies.

God has compassions and comforts in store even for those whom He Himself has grieved. We must be far from thinking that, though God causes grief, the world will relieve and help us. No; the very same that caused the grief must bring in the favor. The same hand inflicted the wound and healed it. He has torn, and He will heal us (Hos. 6:1). When God returns to deal graciously with us, it will not be according to our merits, but according to His mercies, according to the multitude, the abundance, of His mercies. So unworthy we are that nothing but an abundant mercy will relieve us. And God's causing our grief ought to be no discouragement at all to those expectations.

Day 150

When no one else will, nor can, nor dare to shelter me, the Lord is my defense, to preserve me from the evil of my troubles, from sinking under them and being ruined by them. He is the rock of my refuge, in the clefts of which I may take shelter, and on the top of which I may set my feet, to be out of the reach of danger. God is His people's refuge, to whom they may flee, in whom they are safe and may be secure. He is the rock of their refuge, so strong, so firm, impregnable, immovable, as a rock.

> **Psalm 94:22 KJV**
>
> *But the LORD is my defence; and my God is the rock of my refuge.*

Day 151

> **II Corinthians 9:8 KJV**
>
> *And God is able to make all grace abound toward you; that ye, always having all sufficiency in all things, may abound to every good work.*

By "all grace," we are led more fully into the knowledge of His gospel to carry on the work of His grace in the soul and to call forth grace into actions.

There is an increase in gifts bestowed, not only in merely temporal blessings of every sort, which men are unworthy of, but also in all the gifts of God's goodness. These are given to His people in a covenant way, which He can and often does increase. God is able, and He will, and it ought to be believed that He will, cause us to return with an increase, all that which is expended in relieving the necessities of the saints. And, God is able to increase, and will so increase your worldly substance, so that you shall have a sufficiency, a perfect and entire sufficiency, enough for yourselves and families and the relief of the poor, which shall give you satisfaction and contentment, and that at all times, and with respect to everything necessary for you, as to food and clothing, that so you may abound to every good work and to every branch of it, as feeding the hungry and clothing the naked.

Day 152

The vast earth neither rests upon any pillars nor hangs upon any axles. By the almighty power of God, it is firmly fixed in its place, poised with its own weight.

Job 26:7 ESV

He stretches out the north over the void and hangs the earth on nothing.

Oh, how awesome our God is! The art of man could not hang a feather upon anything, yet the divine wisdom hangs the whole earth so. It is poised by its own weight, so says the poet; it is upheld by the Word of God's power, so says the apostle. What is hung upon nothing may serve us to set our feet on and bear the weight of our bodies, but it will never serve us to set our hearts on, nor bear the weight of our souls. These we place in the trust of the Lord.

Day 153

Romans 13:1 AMP

Let every person be loyally subject to the governing (civil) authorities. For there is no authority except from God [by His permission, His sanction], and those that exist do so by God's appointment.

*I*t is of God's ordering that there should be human governments and human laws. Without them there could be no order, security, or progress among mankind. Imperfect as they may often be, and in some instances oppressive and unjust, still they exist for a purpose of good, and form part of the Divine order for the government of the world. In this sense, all are from God and ordained of God; and in submitting to them, we are submitting to God.

Day 154

There is no greater enemy to Christian love than pride and passion. If we do things in contradiction to our brethren, this is doing them through strife. If we do them through ostentation of ourselves, this is doing them through vain-glory: both are

> **Philippians 2:3 NKJV**
>
> *Let nothing **be done** through selfish ambition or conceit, but in lowliness of mind let each esteem others better than himself.*

destructive of Christian love and kindle unchristian contentions. Christ came to slay all enmities; therefore, let there not be among Christians a spirit of opposition. Christ came to humble us, and therefore, let there not be among us a spirit of pride. We must esteem others in lowliness of mind better than ourselves, be severe upon our own faults and charitable in our judgments of others, be quick in observing our own defects and infirmities, but ready to overlook and make favorable allowances for the defects of others. We must esteem the good, which is in others above that which is in ourselves, for we best know our own unworthiness and imperfections. We must interest ourselves in the concerns of others, not in a way of curiosity and severe criticism, or as busybodies in other men's matters, but in Christian love and sympathy.

Day 155

I Corinthians 12:14 KJV

For the body is not one member, but many.

Christ and His church making one body, with Christ as the head and believers making up the various other parts of the body. This body is made up of many parts or members, yet but one body; for all the members are baptized into the same body, and made to drink of the same Spirit. Jews and Gentiles, bond and free, are upon a level in this: all are baptized into the same body, and made partakers of the same Spirit. Christians become members of this body by baptism: they are baptized into one body.

Day 156

*W*e must live a life of self-denial, mortification, and contempt of the world. We must not indulge our ease and appetite, for then it will be hard to bear toil, and weariness, and want, for Christ. We are daily subject to affliction, and we must accommodate ourselves to it, and acquiesce in the will of God in it and learn to endure hardship. We frequently meet crosses in the way

> **Luke 9:23 KJV**
>
> *And he said to them all, If any man will come after me, let him deny himself, and take up his cross daily, and follow me.*

of duty. Though we must not pull them upon our own heads, yet, when they are laid for us, we must take them up, carry them after Christ, and make the best of them.

Day 157

> **Psalm 92:14 KJV**
>
> *They shall still bring forth fruit in old age; they shall be fat and flourishing.*

The products of sanctification, all the instances of a lively devotion and a useful conversation, good works, by which God is glorified and others are edified are the fruits of righteousness, in which it is the privilege, as well as the duty, of the righteous to abound. Their abounding in them is the matter of a promise as well as of a command. It is promised that they shall bring forth fruit in old age. Other trees, when they are old, leave off bearing, but in God's trees, the strength of grace does not fail with the strength of nature. The last days of the saints are sometimes their best days, and their last work is their best work. This indeed shows that they are upright; perseverance is the surest evidence of sincerity.

Day 158

The purpose of this passage is to show God is the owner of all goods. His propriety in it is absolute, sovereign, and unlimited. He may therefore give or withhold His blessings, as He pleases. We have a tendency to determine what a person should rightfully have. In our minds, we wonder *How did he/she get that? Or, Why did he/she get that? or even, Why did they get it and I did not?* But, the right to decide who will obtain the Lord's favor and

> **Matthew 20:14 NIV**
>
> *Take your pay and go. I want to give the one who was hired last the same as I gave you.*

when is solely the Lord's. We do not have a problem when we receive the blessings of God in our life, but we are quick to question or frown upon the blessings of others. If you have ever done so, ask yourself, "Is this the spirit of Christ that I am demonstrating?" If you are honest with yourself, you will answer, "No."

Day 159

Psalm 104:25 LEB

How many are your works, O Yahweh; all of them you have done in wisdom. The earth is full of your creatures.

The psalmist marvels at the works of God. Works of art made by human hands appear rough and unperfected the more closely they are viewed. However, the works of the Lord are all made in wisdom, for they all answer the end they were designed to serve. They are perfect!

Day 160

The apostles made it their business to preach Christ, and not themselves: *We, ministers and believers of today,*

> ### II Corinthians 4:5 KJV
> *For we preach not ourselves, but Christ Jesus the Lord; and ourselves your servants for Jesus' sake.*

should be careful to do the same and not preach ourselves. We should refrain from giving our own notions, private opinions, our passions and prejudices in place of the Word and will of God. We should not seek ourselves, to advance our own secular interest or glory. But we must *preach Christ Jesus the Lord*, as we are Christ's servants. Our business is to make Jesus known to the world as the Messiah, the Christ of God, the only Savior of men.

Day 161

James 4:6 KJV

But he giveth more grace. Wherefore he saith, God resisteth the proud, but giveth grace unto the humble.

The proud resists God: in his understanding, he resists the truths of God; in his will, he resists the truths of God; in his will, he resists the laws of God; in his passions, he resists the providence of God. No wonder God sets Himself against the proud. We should, therefore, resist pride in our hearts, if we do not want God to resist us. While God resists the proud, He gives grace to the humble. And wherever God gives true grace, He will give more. He will especially give more grace to the humble because they see their need of it, will pray for it, and be thankful for it.

Day 162

If any of us thirsts, whoever we may be, we are invited to Christ, whether we are high or low, rich or poor, young or old, bond or free, Jew or Gentile. It is a very gracious initiation to invite us to drink when we thirst. If we desire to be truly and eternally happy, let us apply ourselves to

> **John 7:37 KJV**
>
> *In the last day, that great day of the feast, Jesus stood and cried, saying, If any man thirst, let him come unto me, and drink.*

Christ, and be ruled by Him, and He will take care to make us so.

Day 163

> **Revelation 12:11 KJV**
>
> *And they overcame him by the blood of the Lamb, and by the word of their testimony; and they loved not their lives unto the death.*

The servants of God overcame Satan, by the blood of the Lamb. Christ, by dying, destroyed the devil that has the power of death. By the word of their testimony, as the great instrument of war, the sword of the Spirit, which is the Word of God, by a resolute powerful preaching of the everlasting gospel, which is mighty, through God, to pull down strongholds, and by their courage and patience in sufferings; they loved not their lives unto the death, when the love of life stood in competition with their loyalty to Christ; they loved not their lives so well, but they could give them up to death, could lay them down in Christ's cause; their love to their own lives was overcome by stronger affections of another nature; and this their courage and zeal helped to confound their enemies, to convince many of the spectators, to confirm the souls of the faithful, and so contributed greatly to this victory.

Day 164

*K*eep yourselves in the love of God, the love by which God loves His people. We are exhorted to keep ourselves in it, to set it always before us, to keep it constantly in view, to exercise faith on it, firmly believing our interest in it. We

> **Jude 1:21 KJV**
>
> *Keep yourselves in the love of God, looking for the mercy of our Lord Jesus Christ unto eternal life.*

must also meditate on it, give ourselves up wholly to the contemplation of it, and employ our thoughts constantly about it, which is the foundation of all grace here and glory hereafter. We are to preserve ourselves by it, against Satan's temptations, the snares of the world, and the lusts of the flesh. Whenever Satan solicits us to sin and any snare is laid to draw into it and the flesh attempts to be predominant, we should take ourselves to the love of God and preserve ourselves from sin. It would not be wise to depend on anything that can be done by men; nor is there any danger of real believers falling from it, or losing it, since it is unchangeable, and is from everlasting to everlasting; or else by the love of God we are to understand that love with which His people love Him and of which He is the object (Luke 11:42) (Adapted from John Gill's Exposition of the Entire Bible).

Day 165

> **I Cor. 15:58 KJV**
>
> *Therefore, my beloved brethren, be ye stedfast, unmoveable, always abounding in the work of the Lord, forasmuch as ye know that your labour is not in vain in the Lord.*

I Corinthians 15:58 is an exhortation for believers to be steadfast: firm in the faith of the gospel. Also, for us to be unmovable: in our hope and expectation of the great privilege of being raised incorruptible and immortal in eternity. And to abound in the work of the Lord: always doing the Lord's service and obeying the Lord's commands. May Christ give us faith and increase our faith, that we may not only be safe but joyful and triumphant.

Day 166

The Lord keeps the feet of His saints from falling. He will not suffer them to be moved out of the spiritual estate in which they stand, nor off of the Foundation and Rock of ages, on which their feet are set, and their goings

> **Psalm 121:3 ESV**
>
> *He will not let your foot be moved; he who keeps you will not slumber.*

established; nor out of the house of God, where they are as pillars; nor out of His ways, where He upholds their goings.

Our God who keeps us will not slumber. The Lord God Himself is the keeper of every individual saint, of every regenerate person, of every one of His sheep, of every member of His church. He keeps us by His power, and He preserves us by His grace. He holds us with His right hand, guides us by His counsel, keeps us feet from falling, and brings us safe to glory. For, He is a watchful keeper. He keeps us night and day, so no harm should befall us.

Day 167

Luke 6:31 NLT

Do to others as you would like them to do to you.

One would think this verse would be one of the easiest to adhere to. It does not take great psychology or theology, only common courtesy. The verse simply says to extend the same common courtesy to others that you would like for yourself. However, the expected treatment from others that we have for ourselves doesn't seem to equate with how we treat others. Some people walk through life with a superiority complex as if though they are above others and should therefore be treated better than others. The Bible says God is no respecter of persons. So, then why are we? Why do we respect ourselves above the level of respect we give to others? It is time for a self-check. We need to check our negative attitudes at the door and begin to look through the eyes of love and mutual respect.

Day 168

*B*ecause our hearts are desperately wicked (Jeremiah 17:9) and our spirit and soul are housed in a fleshly body that is prone to sin, we must be careful and diligent about being sure that we do not house evil in our hearts. The result will be turning away from God. Turning away from God is a result of evil leading

> **Hebrews 3:12 NLT**
>
> *Be careful then, dear brothers and sisters. Make sure that your own hearts are not evil and unbelieving, turning you away from the living God.*

to unbelief- pure skepticism. These feelings will exclude us from entering into a heavenly rest with the Lord God.

Day 169

> **Revelation 21:7 KJV**
>
> *He that overcometh shall inherit all things; and I will be his God, and he shall be my son.*

*H*e who overcomes is one who overcomes all spiritual enemies, sin, Satan, and the world, the antichristian beast, his image, mark, and number of his name, one who is more than a conqueror through Christ, and one who perseveres to the end, notwithstanding all temptations, trials, and difficulties. The overcomer shall inherit all things: the kingdom of Christ in the new Jerusalem state, and all things in it, including heaven, eternal glory and happiness, and everlasting salvation. In the coming new and glorious state of things, it will be abundantly manifest that overcomers are the sons of God and seed of Christ. And, it will be known how glorious they are, and shall be, when they shall see Christ in His glory, and be like Him.

Day 170

"*My* grace is sufficient for thee." The Lord always hears and answers His people sooner or later, in one form or another, though not always in the way and manner they desire; but yet in such a way as is most for His glory and their good. Apostle Paul did not have his request granted, that

> **II Cor. 12:9 KJV**
>
> *And he said unto me, My grace is sufficient for thee: for my strength is made perfect in weakness. Most gladly therefore will I rather glory in my infirmities, that the power of Christ may rest upon me.*

Satan might immediately depart from him, only he is assured of a sufficiency of grace to support him under the exercise, so long as it should last. There seems to be an allusion to the word "Shaddai," an appellation of God (Genesis 17:1), and signifies, "which is sufficient," for God is all sufficient and is a name that belongs to the Messiah.

Day 171

I Corinthians 15:4-6 NIV
Christ was buried, that he was raised on the third day according to the Scriptures, and that he appeared to Cephas, and then to the Twelve. After that, he appeared to more than five hundred of the brothers and sisters at the same time, most of whom are still living, though some have fallen asleep.

The doctrine of Christ's death and resurrection is the foundation of Christianity. Remove this and all our hopes for eternity sink at once. And it is by holding this truth firm that Christians stand in the day of trial and are kept faithful to God. We believe in vain, unless we keep in the faith of the gospel. This truth is confirmed by Old Testament prophecies; many saw Christ after He was risen. When sinners are, by divine grace, turned into saints, God causes the remembrance of former sins to make them humble, diligent, and faithful. True believers, though not ignorant of what the Lord has done for, in, and by them, yet when they look at their whole conduct and their obligations, they are led to feel that none are so worthless as they are. All true Christians believe that Jesus Christ, and Him crucified, and then risen from the dead, is the sum and substance of Christianity.

Day 172

*W*hen Christ calls Himself the light, He is expressing He Himself is most excellent and glorious and what He is to the world - the fountain of light, enlightening every man. What a desolate and dark place the world would be without the sun! So would it be without Christ by whom light came into the world to rid mankind of

> ### John 8:12 NASB
>
> *Then Jesus again spoke to them, saying, "I am the Light of the world; he who follows Me will not walk in the darkness, but will have the Light of life."*

darkness. If Christ is the light, then it is our duty as believers to *follow Him*, to submit ourselves to His guidance, and in everything take directions from Him, in the way that leads to happiness. Many follow *false lights* that lead them to destruction; but Christ is the *true light*. It is not enough to *look at* this light, and to *gaze* upon it, but we must follow it, believe in it, and walk in it, for it is a light to *our feet*, not *our eyes* only.

Day 173

Romans 16:3-4 KJV

Greet Priscilla and Aquila my helpers in Christ Jesus: Who have for my life laid down their own necks: unto whom not only I give thanks, but also all the churches of the Gentiles.

Romans 13:7 says to give to those what is due them. In Romans 16:3-4, Apostle Paul is honoring Priscilla and Aquila for the service they have rendered unto him and unto other believers. To whom is honor due in your life? Don't withhold the honor; be gracious and obedient to God's Word and issue the honor that is due. Encourage, love, and respect are great tools for edifying members of the body of Christ.

Day 174

*L*et the words of our mouths, whether it is our speech in common conversation (which should not be filthy, foolish, rotten or corrupt) or our address to God (both in prayer and thanksgiving) and the meditation of our hearts (our inward thoughts continually

Psalm 19:14 KJV

Let the words of my mouth, and the meditation of my heart, be acceptable in thy sight, O LORD, my strength, and my redeemer.

revolving in our mind, our meditation on the Word of God and divine things, or mental prayer) be acceptable in the sight of God. As believers, we are to be a sweet-smelling savor unto the Lord's nostrils. We are to honor, worship and praise Him, through our speech, our thoughts and through our actions.

Day 175

Colossians 3:12-14 NIV

Therefore, as God's chosen people, holy and dearly loved, clothe yourselves with compassion, kindness, humility, gentleness and patience. Bear with each other and forgive one another if any of you has a grievance against someone. Forgive as the Lord forgave you. And over all these virtues put on love, which binds them all together in perfect unity.

As the elect of God, we are to be merciful, not in merely in our actions, but in spirit and affection. In all cases of this kind, let your heart dictate to your hand; be clothed with bowels of mercy – we are to let our most tender feelings come in contact with the miseries of the distressed as soon as ever they present themselves to us.

Day 176

*C*hrist is an awesome example of how to navigate through our earthly walk. He came not to be ministered unto but to minister, to be a servant. He was sent and came as the servant of the Lord; and he ministered, in his prophetic office, the Gospel unto

> **Mark 10:45 ESV**
>
> *For even the Son of Man came not to be served but to serve, and to give his life as a ransom for many.*

men. He went about in the form of a servant, doing good, ministering medicine both to the souls and bodies of men. But, the great work He came to do was the work of man's redemption, which He willingly and cheerfully undertook, diligently and faithfully prosecuted, and has completely finished. He gave His life a ransom for many; even for all the elect of God, to redeem them from sin, Satan, and the law; and secure them from the wrath of God, and eternal death; and this He has done, by laying down His life as the ransom price for them.

Day 177

> **Psalm 119:160 HCSB**
>
> *The entirety of Your word is truth, and all Your righteous judgments endure forever.*

*E*very word from Genesis (called so by the Jews from its first words, 'In the beginning') to the end of the Scriptures is true. Inasmuch we are told to accept, abide, and adhere to all of God's Word, not adding and not subtracting.

Day 178

As believers, we are to love each other for Christ's sake, and according to His example, seek what might benefit others, and promoting the cause of the gospel, as one body, animated by one soul. But

> **John 13:34 NASB**
>
> *A new commandment I give to you, that you love one another, even as I have loved you, that you also love one another.*

this commandment still appears to be difficult and challenging for many. Men, in general, notice and take heed to many of Christ's words rather than these. By doing so it appears, if the followers of Christ do not show love one to another, they give cause to suspect their sincerity and love for Christ Himself and His Word.

Day 179

Romans 7:6 KJV

But now we are delivered from the law, that being dead wherein we were held; that we should serve in newness of spirit, and not in the oldness of the letter.

Being no longer bound to the law, but moving freely in the grace of God, we should serve God in the newness of spirit. That is, in the spirit of godly love, with all diligence, long suffering, and patience. We should walk in meekness and humility, humbling ourselves willingly under the mighty hand of God.

Day 180

*M*inisters of the gospel are not only the servants of Christ Jesus, but also of the churches for His sake. In serving the body, they serve Christ. It is not that they are to be the servants of men and to

> **Mark 10:44 KJV**
>
> *And whosoever of you will be the chiefest, shall be servant of all.*

take their instructions from them and act according to rules prescribed by them, or seek to please men for then they would not be the servants of Christ, but they become servants to *all* that they may win souls to Christ and increase His churches and enlarge His interest.

Day 181

> **I John 4:10 KJV**
>
> *Herein is love, not that we loved God, but that he loved us, and sent his Son to be the propitiation for our sins.*

The love God has for His people existed before the love the people have for Him. When His people were without love for Him, being enemies in their minds, by wicked works, and even enmity itself, He yet loved them. Their love to Him is caused by His love to them. Therefore, His love, and a continuance in it, does not depend on theirs, nor does it vary according to theirs. As a result, there is good reason to believe God's love will continue and will never be removed, as it is not predicated upon His people loving Him first or in return. This unrequited love shows the sovereignty and freeness of the love of God, and that it is surprising and matchless by any other.

Day 182

Death is a great loss to a carnal, worldly man, for he loses all his earthly comforts and all his hopes. But to a true believer it is gain, for it is the end of all his weakness and misery. It delivers him from all

> **Philippians 1:21-23 NIV**
>
> *For to me to live is Christ, and to die is gain. If I am to live in the flesh, that means fruitful labor for me. Yet which I shall choose I cannot tell. I am hard pressed between the two. My desire is to depart and be with Christ,*

the evils of life and brings him to possess the chief good. The apostle's difficulty was not between living in this world and living in heaven; between these two there is no comparison but between serving Christ in this world and enjoying Him in another. Not between two evil things, but between two good things; living to Christ and being with Him. The power of faith and of Divine grace can make us willing to die. In this world, we are compassed with sin; but when with Christ, we shall escape sin and temptation, sorrow and death, forever. But those who have most reason to desire to depart should be willing to remain in the world as long as God has any work for them to do. And the more unexpected mercies are before they come, the more of God will be seen in them.

Day 183

> **Luke 12:15 ISV**
>
> *Then he told them, "Be careful to guard yourselves against every kind of greed, because a person's life doesn't consist of the amount of possessions he has."*

The Word of God clearly tells us that God will give us the desire of our hearts. There is no limit as to what God can and will provide unto His people. However, as believers, we are to take heed and beware of covetousness and the want of possessions for notoriety. Our lives do not consist of the abundance of the things which we possess. Our natural lives cannot be prolonged by all the good things of the world nor can they prevent diseases or death. Also, the comforts and happiness of life do not exist within these things. Our spiritual lives are not advantaged by our possessions and neither is our eternal life attained by the possession of worldly possessions. Let us focus on storing up treasures in heaven because earthly possessions and treasures are temporal.

Day 184

Being in Adam as his natural descendants by him being the first man, we have all sinned in him, and so will die in him. The sentence of

> **I Cor. 15:22 ESV**
>
> *For as in Adam all die, so also in Christ shall all be made alive.*

death passed onto us from him. We are now subject to a bodily death, which has ever since reigned over mankind sin Adam's and Eve's sin in the garden of Eden. At the same time, all that are in Christ that belong to Him, who are His spiritual seed and offspring, to whom He is a covenant head and representative, shall be raised to an immortal life by Him. All the elect of God who have died in Adam or will die will all be quickened or raised to life in and by Christ, for He is the giver of eternal life.

Day 185

> **Proverbs 19:20 ESV**
>
> *Listen to advice and accept instruction, that you may gain wisdom in the future.*

Many people want wisdom without heeding wise counsel. To gain wisdom, we must hear counsel and receive instruction of parents, masters, and ministers, especially the counsel and instruction of Wisdom, of Jesus Christ, the Wisdom of God, the wonderful Counselor, and of his Gospel and of the Scriptures, which are able to make a man wise unto salvation. At death, it will appear abundantly clear as to whether or not man was wise enough to be concerned for a future state, for the good of his soul in another world, by listening to the counsel and instruction of Christ, in His Word, by looking to Him, and believing in Him, for life and salvation, by leaning and living upon Him, and committing the affairs of his soul, and the salvation of it, to Him.

Day 186

Beware that you do not forget the Lord thy God. The Father of mercies and fountain of goodness is the author and giver of every good and perfect gift. When a person walks in abundance, he/she is apt to

> **Deuteronomy 8:11 KJV**
>
> *Beware that thou forget not the LORD thy God, in not keeping his commandments, and his judgments, and his statutes, which I command thee this day.*

forget the goodness of God, when on the contrary one would think the abundance of blessings would keep him/her in continual remembrance of the Supplier and engage to daily thankfulness to Him. In not keeping His commandments, His judgments, and His statutes, which we are commanded this day, God is forgotten.

Day 187

> **I John 4:4 NIV**
>
> *You, dear children, are from God and have overcome them, because the one who is in you is greater than the one who is in the world.*

You have overcome the world's deceivers and their temptations, and there is good ground of hope that you will do so still. The ability to overcome is not within and of ourselves. There is a strong preserver within you: *Because greater is He that is in you than he that is in the world.* The Spirit of God dwells in you, and that Spirit is mightier than men of devils. It is a great happiness to be under the influence of the Holy Ghost. You are not of the same temper with these deceivers. The Spirit of God has framed your mind for God and heaven, *but they are of the world.* The spirit that prevails in them leads them to this world; their heart is addicted; they study the pomp, the pleasure, and interest of the world: *and therefore they speak of the world*; they profess a worldly messiah and savior; they project a worldly kingdom and dominion; the possessions and treasures of the world would they engross to themselves, forgetting that the true Redeemer's *kingdom is not of this world.*

Day 188

*W*e are in this world as a ship at sea, liable to be tossed up and down, and in danger of being cast away. Our souls are the vessels. The comforts, expectations, graces, and happiness of our souls are the precious cargo with which

> **Hebrews 6:19 KJV**
>
> *Which hope we have as an anchor of the soul, both sure and stedfast, and which entereth into that within the veil.*

these vessels are loaded. Heaven is the harbor to which we sail. The temptations, persecutions, and afflictions that we encounter, are the winds and waves that threaten our shipwreck. We have need of an anchor to keep us sure and steady, or we are in continual danger. Gospel hope is our anchor; as in our day of battle, it is our helmet, so in our stormy passage through this world, it is our anchor. It is sure and steadfast, or else it could not keep us so (Matthew Henry Commentary).

Day 189

Proverbs 8:13 KJV

The fear of the LORD is to hate evil: pride, and arrogancy, and the evil way, and the froward mouth, do I hate.

True religion, consisting in the fear of the Lord, which is the wisdom before recommended, teaches men to hate all sin, as it is displeasing to God and destructive to the soul. The fear of the Lord is to hate evil, the evil way, to hate sin as sin, and therefore, to hate every false way. Wherever there is an awe of God, there is a dread of sin, as an evil, as only evil, particularly to hate pride and passion, those two common and dangerous sins. Conceitedness of ourselves, pride and arrogancy, are sins which Christ hates, and so do all those who have the Spirit of Christ. Everyone hates them in others, but we must hate them in ourselves. The froward mouth, peevishness towards others, God hates, because it is such an enemy to the peace of mankind, and therefore, we should hate it. Be it spoken to the honor of religion that however it is unjustly accused, it is so far from making men conceited and sour that there is nothing more directly contrary to it than pride and passion, nor which it teaches us more to detest.

Day 190

> **Hebrews 12:1-2 KJV**
>
> *Wherefore seeing we also are compassed about with so great a cloud of witnesses, let us lay aside every weight, and the sin which doth so easily beset us, and let us run with patience the race that is set before us, Looking unto Jesus the author and finisher of our faith; who for the joy that was set before him endured the cross, despising the shame, and is set down at the right hand of the throne of God.*

This race is set before them; it is marked out unto them, both by the Word of God and the examples of the faithful servants of God, that cloud of witnesses with which they are compassed about. It is set out by proper limits and directions; the mark they run to, and the prize they run for, are set before them. This race must be run with patience and perseverance. There will be need of patience to encounter the difficulties that lie in our way, of perseverance to resist all temptations to desist or turn aside. Faith and patience are the conquering graces, and therefore must be always cultivated and kept in lively exercise.

Day 191

Ephesians 3:20 KJV

Now unto him that is able to do exceeding abundantly above all that we ask or think, according to the power that worketh in us.

When the things we are facing in our lives loom so big in our eyes that our mind goes "tilt," we need to think in the spirit. In the natural, many things are impossible. But in the supernatural, the spiritual realm, with God nothing is impossible. God wants us to believe for great things, make big plans, and expect Him to do things so great that it leaves us with our mouths hanging open in awe. James 4:2 tells us we have not because we ask not! We can be bold in our asking (Joyce Meyer).

Day 192

God has promised to meet your financial needs. He's just waiting for you to ask for His help! The Lord never shuts His storehouse until you shut your mouth. One of the reasons why we see so few miracles in our lives is because we just don't ask for them. Instead of living a life based on Christ, we live a life

> **John 16:24 NCV**
>
> *You have not asked for anything in my name. Ask and you will receive, so that your joy will be the fullest possible joy.*

based on credit. When we have something we need in our life, instead of stopping and asking God for it, before we even *think* about asking God for it, we just use a credit card. We trust credit instead of Christ. Do you know why God wants you to learn to ask for things in prayer? So, He can give them, and so, you'll be full of joy. God is a loving father. He's not some ogre sitting in the sky, waiting to make your life a bummer. He wants to bless your life! You just have to ask (Rick Warren).

Day 193

*L*istening is the first step in acting out the scriptures, not speaking. The church has the potential to do so much good in the world, to share the love of Christ with so many people. However, in order to do this, we must first stop talking, sit quietly, and get to know them. We need to hear their stories, understand their hurts, empathize with their anger, and then, when they have nothing else to say, that is when we speak our truth. It's time to start using our ears before we use our words (Ryan Duncan).

> **Proverbs 12:15 ESV**
>
> *The way of a fool is right in his own eyes, but a wise man listens to advice.*

Day 194

*T*he 'Word of God,' whether the verse is referring to Jesus (John 1:1) or the Word itself, is *quick*; it is very lively and active, in all its efforts, in seizing the conscience of sinners, in cutting them to the heart, and in comforting them and binding up the wounds of the soul. Those who call the Word

> **Hebrews 4:12 KJV 2000**
>
> *For the word of God is living and powerful! It is sharper than any two-edged sword, piercing to the dividing of soul and spirit, and of the joints and marrow, and is a discerner of the thoughts and intentions of the heart.*

of God a dead letter or an outdated book do not fully know it or understand it. Saints die, and sinners die, but the Word of God lives. Matthew 5:18 states, not one jot or tittle of God's Word will pass away, even if heaven and earth do.

Day 195

> **2 Timothy 3:16-17 KJV**
>
> *All scripture is given by inspiration of God, and is profitable for doctrine, for reproof, for correction, for instruction in righteousness that the man of God may be perfect, thoroughly furnished unto all good works.*

*A*ll Scripture is divine revelation, which we may depend upon as infallibly true. The same Spirit that breathed reason into us breathes revelation among us. The prophets and apostles did not speak from themselves, but that which they received of the Lord that they delivered unto us. The Word of God is a sure guide in our way to eternal life. The scriptures are able to make us truly wise, wise for our souls and another world. It is profitable to us for all the purposes of the Christian life, for doctrine, for reproof, for correction, for instruction in righteousness. It answers all the ends of divine revelation. It instructs us in that which is true, reproves us for that which is amiss, and directs us in that which is good. It is of use to all, for we all need to be instructed, corrected, and reproved: it is of special use to ministers, who are to give instruction, correction, and reproof. Mankind is perfected by the Word of God in this world by Scripture. By it, we are thoroughly furnished for every good work.

Day 196

*A*sk- represent your wants and burdens to God, and refer yourselves to Him for support and supply, according to His promises. *Seek by prayer*, as for a thing of value that we have lost. *Knock*, as one that desires to enter into a house would knock at the door. In doing so,

> **Matthew 7:7-8 WEB**
>
> *Ask, and it will be given to you. Seek, and you will find. Knock, and the door will be opened to you. For everyone who asks, receives; and he who seeks, finds; and to him who knocks, the door will be opened.*

you would be admitted to converse with God and taken into His love and favor. By prayer, we knock. Christ knocks at our door (Rev. 3:20) and allows us to knock at His. Seeking and knocking imply something more than asking and praying. We must not only ask but seek; we must second our prayers with our endeavors; we must, in the use of the appointed means, seek for that which we ask for.

Day 197

Isaiah 30:19 WEB

For the people will dwell in Zion at Jerusalem; you will weep no more, for Yahweh will be gracious to you; He will hear the voice of your cry and answer you.

God will be very gracious. He will hear the cry of our lips springing forth from our hearts. He will be gracious to answer us, and our needs will exist no more. Those who were in tears will have cause to rejoice and shall weep no more; and those who dwell in Zion, the holy city, will find enough there to wipe away tears from their eyes.

Day 198

Christ encourages us to come to God in all circumstances, with all our supplications and requests. Through Him, our petitions are admitted and accepted of God. The substance of our prayer must be in agreement with the declared will of God. It is not fit that we should ask what is contrary either to His majesty and glory or to our own good, as we are His and are dependent upon Him. When we operate in accordance to His will, we may have confidence that our prayers of faith will be heard in heaven. Knowing that our petitions are heard or accepted is as good as knowing they are answered.

> **1 John 5:14-15 ISV**
>
> *And this is the confidence that we have in him: if we ask for anything according to his will, he listens to us. And if we know that he listens to our requests, we can be sure that we have what we ask him for.*

Day 199

> **Psalm 145:18-19 ESV**
>
> *The LORD is near to all who call on him, to all who call on him in truth. He fulfills the desire of those who fear him; he also hears their cry and saves them.*

*G*od is very ready to hear and answer the prayers of His people. He will be always within earshot of our prayers, and we will always find ourselves within reach of His help. We are to fear Him, worship and serve Him with a holy awe of Him and call upon Him in truth. For, He desires truth in the inward part. We must be faithful to God and sincere in our professions of dependence on Him and devotedness to Him. That which lies within us must be exercised by our daily actions. Namely, we must be doers of His Word and not just professors.

Day 200

*B*ut without faith it is impossible to please Him, or do things well pleasing in His sight; or any of the duties of religion, in an acceptable way; as prayer, praise, attendance on the Word and ordinances, or any good works whatever; because such are without

> **Hebrews 11:6 NIV**
>
> *And without faith it is impossible to please God, because anyone who comes to him must believe that he exists and that he rewards those who earnestly seek him.*

Christ, and without His Spirit; and have neither right principles, nor right ends: for this is not to be understood of the persons of God's elect, as considered in Christ; in whom they are well pleasing to Him before faith; being loved by Him with an everlasting love; and chosen in Christ, before the foundation of the world (Gill's Exposition of the Entire Bible).

Day 201

Romans 10:17 AKJV

So then faith comes by hearing, and hearing by the word of God.

𝓕aith is a result of hearing. This verse is the summary of what Paul said in the prior verses. The beginning, progress, and strength of faith are by hearing. The Word of God is therefore called the Word of faith: it leads to and nourishes faith. God gives faith, but it is by the Word as the instrument. Hearing (that hearing which works faith) is by the Word of God. It is not hearing the enticing words of man's wisdom, but hearing the Word of God, that will befriend faith, and hearing it as the Word of God.

Day 202

*W*e are to confess our faults to one another when we have committed a fault against another believer. However, we are to confess our sins before God. Our confessing is to receive the forgiveness Christ's shed blood paid for on Calvary's cross, sins- past, present and

> **1 John 1:9 ESV**
>
> *If we confess our sins, He is faithful and just to forgive us our sins, and to cleanse us from all unrighteousness.*

future. We do, also, need God's grace. When we humble ourselves under the hand of God and confess unto Him; thereby repenting of said sins, we receive His pardon and His grace (unmerited favor).

Day 203

> **Matthew 11:28-30 NIV**
>
> *Come to me, all you who are weary and burdened, and I will give you rest. Take my yoke upon you and learn from me, for I am gentle and humble in heart, and you will find rest for your souls. For my yoke is easy and my burden is light.*

Christ beckons us to come unto Him when we find ourselves weary and loaded down by the cares of this world. When we come, we are promised rest. Jesus Christ will give assured rest to those weary souls that by faith come to Him for it. The rest He promises is a release from the burden of sin, not from the service of God, but an obligation to the duty we owe to Him. Christ has a yoke for our necks, as well as a crown for our heads. He expects us to take this yoke upon us. To take Christ's yoke upon us is to put ourselves into the relation to servants and subjects to Him, and then to conduct ourselves accordingly, in a conscientious obedience to all His commands, in cheerful submission. Because His yoke is easy and His burden is light, we need not be afraid of it, for He cares for us.

Day 204

Becoming a new creature in Christ should be of primary importance of all who profess the Christian faith, having a new heart and new nature. And so great is the change the grace of God makes in the soul that it naturally

> **2 Cor. 5:17 KJV**
>
> *Therefore if any man be in Christ, he is a new creature: old things are passed away; behold, all things are become new.*

follows that old things are passed away - old thoughts, old principles, and old practices, and all these things must become new. The renewed man acts from new principles, by new rules, with new ends, and in new company.

Day 205

> **Isaiah 40:28-31 ASV**
>
> *Hast thou not known? hast thou not heard? The everlasting God, Jehovah, the Creator of the ends of the earth, fainteth not, neither is weary; there is no searching of his understanding. He giveth power to the faint; and to him that hath no might he increaseth strength.*

When we are wise in our weakness and acknowledge we lack the strength to successfully navigate through this life on our own, God increases our strength. When we are weak in ourselves, then are we strong in the Lord. On the contrary, if we trust in our own sufficiency and are so confident of it that we neither exert ourselves to the utmost nor seek unto God for His grace, we are apt to think ourselves to be stronger than we actually are. But if we wait on the Lord, rely upon Him, and commit ourselves to His guidance will find that God will not fail us. He will renew our strength.

Day 206

*I*t is not uncommon for believers to share in the calamities of human life and commonly have a greater share in them than others. As a result, believers shed many tears. *H*owever, weeping must not hinder sowing. Ironically, when we suffer ill,

> **Psalm 126:5-6 KJV**
> *They that sow in tears shall reap in joy. He that goeth forth and weepeth, bearing precious seed, shall doubtless come again with rejoicing, bringing his sheaves with him.*

we must be doing well because the devil does not attempt to hinder those who are part of his army. He targets his focus on those in God's army. But, as a result of their labor, they shall have a harvest of joy. The troubles of the saints will not last always. When they have done their work, they will have a season of joy. Those that sow in the tears of godly sorrow shall reap in the joy of a sealed pardon and a settled peace.

Day 207

Isaiah 43:2-3 ASV

When thou passest through the waters, I will be with thee; and through the rivers, they shall not overflow thee: when thou walkest through the fire, thou shalt not be burned, neither shall the flame kindle upon thee. For I am Jehovah thy God, the Holy One of Israel, thy Saviour; I have given Egypt as thy ransom, Ethiopia and Seba in thy stead.

When we pass through the waters and the rivers, through the fire and the flame, God will be with us and will be our security. When dangers are very imminent and threatening, He will deliver us out of them. Did the Israelites in their journey from the wilderness pass through deep water? They did not perish in it. Should their persecutors cast them into a fiery furnace, for their constant adherence to their God? Yet, the flame did not kindle upon them, which was fulfilled in the letter in the wonderful preservation of the three Hebrew boys. Though they went through fire and water, which would be to them as the valley of the shadow of death, they had God with them. So, they need not fear any evil (Adapted from Matthew Henry's Commentary).

Day 208

The patience of the saints is exhibited in believing in, and waiting for, the due retribution which will overtake the wicked at the last, and in maintaining the conflict against the dragon who goes to war with those

> **Revelation 14:12 KJV**
>
> *Here is the patience of the saints: here are they that keep the commandments of God, and the faith of Jesus.*

"who keep the commandments of God, and have the testimony of Jesus" (Revelation 12:17), the testimony which is the outcome of faith (see also Revelation 13:10) (Pulpit Commentary).

Day 209

John 14:18 KJV

I will not leave you comfortless: I will come to you.

Christ promises He will continue His care of those who follow after Him. He declares, "I will not leave you orphans, or fatherless, for though I leave you, yet I leave you this comfort, I will come to you. I will come speedily to you at my resurrection. I will come daily to you in my Spirit." He will come in the tokens of His love and the visits of His grace. He continues, "I will come certainly at the end of time." Those who see Christ with an eye of faith shall see Him forever; the world sees Him no more until His second coming, but His disciples have communion with Him in His absence.

Day 210

The Lord will be a refuge for the oppressed, a high place, a strong place, in times of trouble. Many of God's people may be oppressed in this world and have

> **Psalm 9:9-10 KJV**
>
> *The LORD also will be a refuge for the oppressed, a refuge in times of trouble. And they that know thy name will put their trust in thee: for thou, LORD, hast not forsaken them that seek thee.*

troublesome times appointed to them. Although God may not immediately appear unto them as their deliverer and avenger in the time frame that they desire, they can still flee to Him as their refuge and depend upon His power for their safety. They have the peace of knowing no real hurt shall be done them. Those who know Him to be a god of infinite wisdom will trust Him further than they can see Him. Those who know Him to be a god of almighty power will trust Him when confidences in man fail and they have nothing else to trust. Those who know him to be a god of infinite grace and goodness will trust Him though He slay them. Those who know Him to be a god of inviolable truth and faithfulness will rejoice in His Word of promise and rest upon that, though the performance is deferred and intermediate providences seem to contradict it.

Day 211

> ### Revelation 21:1-4 KJV
>
> *And I saw a new heaven and a new earth: for the first heaven and the first earth were passed away; and there was no more sea. And I John saw the holy city, new Jerusalem, coming down from God out of heaven, prepared as a bride adorned for her husband. And I heard a great voice out of heaven saying, Behold, the tabernacle of God is with men, and he will dwell with them, and they shall be his people, and God himself shall be with them, and be their God. And God shall wipe away all tears from their eyes; and there shall be no more death, neither sorrow, nor crying, neither shall there be any more pain: for the former things are passed away.*

The new heaven and the new earth will not be separate from each other; the earth of the saints, their glorified bodies, will be heavenly. The old world, with all its troubles and tumults, will have passed away. There will be no sea; this aptly represents freedom from conflicting passions, temptations, troubles, changes, and alarms; from whatever can divide or interrupt the communion of saints. This new Jerusalem is the church of God in its new and perfect state, the church triumphant. No signs, no remembrance of former sorrows shall remain. Christ makes all things new.

Day 212

*G*od is faithful to His covenant and will show mercy and do good to those that love Him. On the contrary, for those who hate Him, He will bring terrible retribution. The people were warned about this in the past, and we are warned of it today. It is imperative that we take heed against rebellion and apostasy from Him.

Deuteronomy 7:9 ESV

Know therefore that the LORD your God is God, the faithful God who keeps covenant and steadfast love with those who love him and keep his commandments, to a thousand generations.

Day 213

Deuteronomy 31:6 HCSB

Be strong and courageous; don't be terrified or afraid of them. For it is the LORD your God who goes with you; He will not leave you or forsake you.

We, as believers and followers of Christ, have His power engaged with us. Therefore, the spirit of fear should not grip our hearts. With God, we can do anything but fail. Remember, He created us to be more than conquerors, a victorious royal priesthood in Christ Jesus. He is an ever-present God, who will never leave or forsake us.

Day 214

$\mathcal{M}$oses assures Israel of the constant presence of God with them. This is applied by the apostle to all God's spiritual Israel, to encourage their faith

> **Deuteronomy 31:8 NIV**
>
> *The LORD himself goes before you and will be with you; he will never leave you nor forsake you. Do not be afraid; do not be discouraged.*

and hope; unto us is this gospel preached, as well as unto them; He will never fail thee, nor forsake thee. Moses commends Joshua to them for a leader; one whose wisdom, courage, and affection they had long known; one whom God had appointed to be their leader, and therefore would own and bless. Joshua is well pleased to be admonished by Moses to be strong and of good courage. Those shall speed well, who have God with them; therefore, they ought to be of good courage. Through God let us do valiantly, for through Him we shall do victoriously; if we resist the devil, he will flee from us.

Day 215

Joshua 1:9 NASV

Have I not commanded you? Be strong and courageous! Do not tremble or be dismayed, for the LORD your God is with you wherever you go.

Throughout scripture, we are often reminded of the characteristics of the god we serve. Our God is a god who will stick with us throughout the good times as well as the bad. Unlike man, who will leave us in the times of trouble, God is prepared to be with us for the long haul. We can take Him at His word that He will never leave us or forsake us. Be encouraged today in whatever trial you may be facing because you have an advocate.

Day 216

*W*e are encouraged in battle. No matter what enemy we may face (backbiting, envy, strife, jealously, hatred, slander, libel, physical attacks, etc.), we are not to fret defeat. We, the righteous of Christ, will be avenged by the almighty God.

> **Joshua 10:25 NIV**
>
> *Joshua said to them, "Do not be afraid; do not be discouraged. Be strong and courageous. This is what the LORD will do to all the enemies you are going to fight."*

Day 217

*W*e are to understand humility, which is opposed to pride.

Ephesians 4:2 NIV

Be completely humble and gentle; be patient, bearing with one another in love.

Patience implies bearing injuries, without seeking revenge. Christians have need to bear one with another, to make the best one of another, to provoke one another's graces and not their passions. Without these things unity cannot be preserved. The first step towards unity is humility; without this there will be no meekness, no patience, or forbearance; and without these no unity. Pride and passion break the peace, and make all the mischief. Humility and meekness restore the peace, and keep it. Only by pride comes contention; only by humility comes love. The more lowly-mindedness, the more like-mindedness. We do not walk worthy of the vocation wherewith we are called if we are not meek and lowly of heart.

Day 218

David is discussing the prophesied death of our Savior and His connection to God. Jesus always did the will of the Father, keeping His eyes always focused on Him. By doing

> **Psalm 16:8 NIV**
>
> *I keep my eyes always on the LORD. With him at my right hand, I will not be shaken.*

so, He knew His adversaries would not shake Him. We should take on this same perspective. When we walk with Christ, we walk in the assurance of His majesty and power. We should constantly remind ourselves of the characteristics of the God we serve: omniscient, omnipresent, and omnipotent. He is the Almighty God, the one true living God, who can do anything but fail!

Day 219

Psalm 27:4 NIV

One thing I ask from the LORD, this only do I seek: that I may dwell in the house of the LORD all the days of my life, to gaze on the beauty of the LORD and to seek him in his temple.

David demonstrates his desire to be in the presence of God. What do you desire today? Do you desire earthly possessions and riches that will give you material wealth? Do you desire to have prestige amongst family, friends, and colleagues? Being in God's presence allows one to walk in the fullness of God. We are told to seek first the kingdom of God and all these things will be added unto us (Matthew 6:33). We must remain focused on our creator and His will. When we do so, He will give us the desires of our heart (Psalm 37:4). We must keep our mind focused on Him, and He will give us peace (Isaiah 26:3).

Day 220

*T*here is nothing like the believing hope of eternal life, the foresights of that glory, and foretastes of those pleasures, to keep us from fainting under all calamities. In the meantime, we should be strengthened to bear

> **Psalm 27:14 NIV**
>
> *Wait for the LORD; be strong and take heart and wait for the LORD.*

up under our burdens. Let us look unto the suffering Savior and pray in faith, not to be delivered into the hands of our enemies. Let us encourage each other to wait on the Lord, with patient expectation and fervent prayer (Matthew Henry Concise Commentary).

Day 221

Psalm 30:6-7 NIV

When I felt secure, I said, "I will never be shaken." LORD, when you favored me, you made my royal mountain stand firm; but when you hid your face, I was dismayed.

David, like many of us, was blinded by his prosperity, the blessings he received from the Lord. He was highly favored of God and began to pay more attention to his material wealth than to the praise and worship of the one who poured out the blessings. When God hid His face from David, David knew He had fallen short and disappointed God. Are you like David? Have you begun to glorify and worship material gains rather than the one who blessed you with them? We must be steadfast and unmovable in our worship of God. He should be our focus at all times, for God is the one who gives us the power to get wealth and not we ourselves (Deuteronomy 8:18).

Day 222

David desired the Lord to lead him in the way of truth and paths of righteousness, according to His Word, and guide him with His counsel, and by His Spirit, that so he might walk in the way in which he should go. This God declares He would do "for His

> **Psalm 31:3 ESV**
>
> *For you are my rock and my fortress; and for your name's sake you lead me and guide me.*

name's sake," not for any merit or worthiness in Him, but for the glory of His own name, and for the honor of His free grace and mercy. Proclaim the Lord to be your protector and your refuge. In honor of His own name, He will be so.

Day 223

> **Psalm 32:8 NIV**
>
> *I will instruct you and teach you in the way you should go; I will counsel you with my loving eye on you.*

*S*ome apply this to God's conduct and direction. He teaches us by His Word and guides us with His eye, by the secret intimations of His will in the hints and turns of Providence, which He enables His people to understand and take direction from, as a master makes a servant know his mind by a wink of his eye. When Christ turned and looked upon Peter, He guided him with His eye. But it is rather to be taken as David's promise to those who sat under his instruction, his own children and family especially: "*I will counsel thee; my eye shall be upon thee.*" "I will give thee the best counsel I can and then observe whether thou takest it or no." Those that are taught in the Word should be under the constant inspection of those that teach them; spiritual guides must be overseers. In this application of the foregoing doctrine concerning the blessedness of those whose sins are pardoned, we have a word to sinners and a word to saints; and this is rightly dividing the Word of truth and giving to each their portion (Matthew Henry's Commentary).

Day 224

"*O*taste and see." Make a trial, an inward, experimental trial of the goodness of God. You cannot see except by tasting for yourself; but if you taste you shall see, for this, like Jonathan's honey, enlightens

> **Psalm 34:8 NIV**
> *Taste and see that the LORD is good; blessed is the one who takes refuge in him.*

the eyes. "That the Lord is good." You can only know this really and personally by experience. There is the banquet with its oxen and fatlings; its fat things full of marrow, and wines on the lees well refined; but their sweetness will be all unknown to you except you make the blessings of grace your own, by a living, inward, vital participation in them. "Blessed is the man that trusteth in him." Faith is the soul's taste; they who test the Lord by their confidence always find Him good, and they become themselves blessed. The second clause of the verse is the argument in support of the exhortation contained in the first sentence (The Treasury of David).

Day 225

Psalm 34:19 KJV

Many are the afflictions of the righteous: but the LORD delivereth him out of them all.

Between the graces of heaven and the malice of hell, believers are very likely to have troubles befall them. This verse assures us that we will. However, the second portion of the verse gives us comfort. No matter what our afflictions are, the Lord our God will deliver us from them.

Day 226

*N*one of those that trust in Him shall be desolate; that is, they shall not be comfortless, for they shall not be cut off from their communion with God. No man is desolate but he whom God has forsaken, nor is any

> **Psalm 34:22 NIV**
>
> *The LORD will rescue his servants; no one who takes refuge in him will be condemned.*

man undone till he is in hell. Those that are God's faithful servants, that make it their care to please Him and their business to honor Him, and in doing so trust Him to protect and reward them, and, with good thoughts of Him, refer themselves to Him, have reason to be easy whatever befalls them, for they are safe and will be happy.

Day 227

> **Psalm 37:4 NIV**
>
> *Take delight in the LORD, and he will give you the desires of your heart.*

*W*e were commanded in Psalm 37:3 to do good, and then follows the command in Verse 4 to delight in God, which is as much a privilege as a duty. If we make conscience of obedience to God, we may then take the comfort of complacency in Him. And even this pleasant duty of delighting in God has a promise annexed to it, which is very full and precious, enough to recompense the hardest services: *He shall give thee the desires of thy heart*. He has not promised to gratify all the appetites of the body and the humors of the fancy, but to grant all the desires of the heart, all the cravings of the renewed sanctified soul. What is the desire of the heart of a good man? It is this, to know, and love, and live to God, to please Him and to be pleased in Him.

Day 228

Bad as the times are, as insulting as our enemies may be, and as hopeless in the sight of man our condition may be, there is yet no room for despair. All things are possible to God. We have a promise of restoration; He is as good as He is powerful; hope therefore in Him. We should yet praise Him, for He is the health of our soul. I shall have the light and help of His countenance, His approbation, and a glorious deliverance by His right hand.

> **Psalm 42:5-6 NIV**
>
> *Why, my soul, are you downcast? Why so disturbed within me? Put your hope in God, for I will yet praise him, my Savior and my God. My soul is downcast within me; therefore I will remember you from the land of the Jordan, the heights of Hermon—from Mount Mizar.*

Day 229

Psalm 46:1-3 NIV

God is our refuge and strength, an ever-present help in trouble. Therefore we will not fear, though the earth give way and the mountains fall into the heart of the sea, though its waters roar and foam and the mountains quake with their surging.

When we are pursued, God is our refuge to whom we may flee and in whom we may be safe. When we are oppressed by troubles, or have work to do and enemies to grapple with, God is our strength, to bear us up under our burdens. When we are in distress, He is a help, to do all that we need. Our God is all-sufficient to us. If God be for us, who can be against us- to do us any harm? It is our duty, it is our privilege, to be thus fearless; it is evidence of a clear conscience, of an honest heart, and of a lively faith in God and His providence and promise.

Day 230

Whatever we find burdensome, we are to lay it upon the Lord. With the wisdom of God, we cast our burdens onto Him. He

> **Psalm 55:22 NIV**
>
> *Cast your cares on the LORD and he will sustain you; he will never let the righteous be shaken.*

shall never suffer the righteous to be moved. We may be moved like the boughs of a tree in a very strong wind, but we shall never be moved like a tree torn up by the roots. When we stand in God, we stand firm. Many would like to destroy the saints, but God will not allow it to come to pass. Like pillars, the godly stand immovable, to the glory of God.

Day 231

Psalm 62:6 KJV
He only is my rock and my salvation: he is my defence; I shall not be moved.

*D*avid viewed God as his rock and his salvation. He knew God alone had the ability to save him. He, as we are, was incapable of saving himself. With that knowledge, David also knew he could trust God to be his defense and his protector. His faith was further developed, and he trusted God the more. No matter what enemy David faced, he knew he would not be overcome. How strong is your faith today? Do you trust God implicitly with your life? What more does God need to do for you to get you to walk totally with Him?

Day 232

*T*hough God works all works of grace for us and in us, there is a work of duty and obedience to Him for us to do. We should not be slothful and inactive when it comes to being obedient to God's commands. Rather, we should be propelled into work by what He has done for us. Our hands should be continually employed in service for His honor and

> **Psalm 90:17 NIV**
> *May the favor of the Lord our God rest on us; establish the work of our hands for us—yes, establish the work of our hands.*

glory. Whatever we find to do, we should do it with all the might of grace we have. We should be steadfast and unmovable, always abounding in the work of the Lord: His love is continuously shown toward us. Will we not return the favor?

Day 233

Psalm 103:2-6 NIV

Praise the LORD, my soul, and forget not all his benefits— who forgives all your sins and heals all your diseases, who redeems your life from the pit and crowns you with love and compassion, who satisfies your desires with good things so that your youth is renewed like the eagle's. The LORD works righteousness and justice for all the oppressed.

*I*n order for us to return praises to God, there must be a grateful remembrance of the mercies we have received from Him. Sin kept good things from us, but our pardon restored us to the favor of God, and now good things are bestowed upon us. When God, by the graces and comforts of His Spirit, recovers His people from their decays and fills them with new life and joy, which is to them an earnest of eternal life and joy, then they may be said to return to the days of their youth.

Day 234

The Lord is my strength and song. It is the Lord who strengthens us, helps us, and gives us the victory. The Lord is the author and giver of strength, natural and spiritual; He is the "strength" of the

> **Psalm 118:14 NIV**
>
> *The LORD is my strength and my defense; he has become my salvation.*

hearts and lives of His people, and of their salvation. Therefore, it is our "song," the matter of it: that we sing of His nature and perfections, of His works of providence and grace, of His righteousness and salvation. He is our salvation, the author of temporal, spiritual, and eternal salvation, so let's sing praises unto Him. (Adapted from John Gill's Commentary).

Day 235

> **Psalm 119:105 KJV**
>
> *Thy word is a lamp unto my feet, and a light unto my path.*

*W*e are walkers through the city of this world, and we are often called to go out into its darkness. Let us never venture there without the light-giving Word, causing us to slip with our feet. Each person should use the Word of God personally, practically, and habitually, so he/she may see his/her way and see what lies in it. When darkness settles down all around us, the Word of the Lord, like a flaming torch, reveals our way. One of the most practical benefits of the Holy Writ is guidance in the acts of daily life; it is not sent to astound us with its brilliance or astound us with confusing words, but to guide us by its instruction. It is true the head needs illumination, but even more the feet need direction; otherwise, head and feet may both fall into a ditch. Blessed are they who personally appropriate God's Word and practically use it as comfort and counselor - a lamp for the feet. It is a lamp by night, a light by day, and a delight at all times. Praise the Lord!

Day 236

God's people are safe under His protection. He is their strength and their shield, their help and their shield, their sun and their shield, their shield and their great reward, and here their hiding

Psalm 119:114-115 NIV

You are my refuge and my shield; I have put my hope in your word. Away from me, you evildoers, that I may keep the commands of my God!

place and their shield. They may by faith retire to Him, and repose in Him as their hiding place, where they are kept in secret. They may by faith oppose His power to all the might and malice of their enemies, as their shield to quench every fiery dart. Those who are to keep God's commandments must be often renewing their resolutions to do so. They say, "They are the commandments of God, of my God, and therefore I will keep them. He is God and may command me, my God and will command me nothing but what is for my good."

Day 237

Psalm 119:25 NIV

I am laid low in the dust; preserve my life according to your word.

When we find ourselves low in spirit, as one who is desolated and lies upon the ground, we can petition the Lord for preservation. In God's Word is life. It breeds hope, peace, joy, laughter, and internal comfort. Don't allow the cares of this world to bog you down. Envelope yourself into the Word of God and allow hope to spring eternal.

Day 238

Every believer has had afflictions; none are without. It is the will of God that so it should be. Many are their afflictions, inward and outward, but the Word of God is

> **Psalm 119:50 NIV**
>
> *My comfort in my suffering is this: Your promise preserves my life.*

often their comfort under them, the written Word, heard or read, especially a word of promise, powerfully applied. When we suffer afflictions, it is imperative to apply the balm of the Word to them. If we strive and commit to hiding God's words in our heart, we can quickly recollect them in our time of need. Never be without the sword. It cuts both ways and will alleviate any affliction.

Day 239

Psalm 119:71 NIV

It was good for me to be afflicted so that I might learn your decrees.

The proud are full of the world and its wealth and pleasures; these make them senseless, secure, and stupid. God visits His people with affliction, so they may learn his statutes. Not only God's promises, but even His law, His precepts. They are desirable and profitable, because they lead us with safety and delight unto eternal life. Those who love God cleave to Him and His Word. When we have troubles, we turn to His Word. When we need more faith, we turn to His Word. When we have questions and need answers, we turn to His Word. His Word is there to assist us in our daily earthly walk and guide us eternally into His loving arms. We will fail to go to God's Word willingly, afflictions will take us there.

Day 240

*S*lander causes distress of the most grievous kind. Those who have felt the edge of a cruel tongue know assuredly that it is sharper than the sword. We can

> **Psalm 120:1 NIV**
>
> *I call on the LORD in my distress, and he answers me.*

ward off the strokes of brutality, but we have no shield against a liar's tongue. We do not know who was the father of the falsehood, nor where it was born, nor where it has gone, nor how to follow it, nor how to stay its withering influence. We are perplexed and know not which way to turn. In such distress, we need not hesitate to cry unto the Lord. Refrain from discussing with man; instead, pray to God. These are the best cures for the evil of slander. It is wisest course that one can follow. It is of little use to appeal to our fellows on the matter of slander, for the more we stir in it, the more it spreads. It is of no avail to appeal to the honor of the slanderers, for they have none, and the most piteous demands for justice will only increase their malignity and encourage them to fresh insult. Let it be! Cry unto the Lord, for He is our refuge!

Day 241

> **Psalm 121:1-2 KJV**
>
> *I will lift up mine eyes unto the hills, from whence cometh my help. My help cometh from the LORD, which made heaven and earth.*

*W*e must not rely upon creatures, upon men and means, instruments and second causes, nor make flesh our weapon. We must see all our help laid up in God, in His power and goodness, His providence and grace. From Him, we must expect our help to come, saying, "My help comes from the Lord; the help I desire is what He sends, and from Him, I expect it in His own way and time. If he does not help, no creature can help; if he does, no creature can hinder, can hurt." We must look to and receive from God, by faith in His promises, for His Word will not return unto Him void. It will accomplish that for which it has been sent!

Day 242

God's protection will keep us safe in every respect: from the evil of sin and the evil of trouble. He will prevent the evil we may fear. He will sanctify, remove, or lighten, the evil we may feel around us. Likewise, He will keep us from doing evil, and far from suffering evil. So,

> **Psalm 121:7-8 ESV**
>
> *The LORD will keep you from all evil; he will keep your life. The LORD will keep your going out and your coming it from this time forth and forevermore.*

whatever afflictions happen to us, there shall be no evil in it. Even the evil that kills will not ultimately hurt, because it is the spiritual life, especially, that God will take under His protection. Man may be able to harm the body, but the soul he cannot destroy.

Day 243

Psalm 145:18-19 NIV

The LORD is near to all who call on him, to all who call on him in truth. He fulfills the desires of those who fear him; he hears their cry and saves them.

God is very ready to hear and answer the prayers of His people. He will always be within call of our prayers, and we shall always find ourselves within reach of His help. If a neighbor that is near is better than a brother afar off, it is even better to have a God that is near. He will not only be near to us to hear, but He will fulfill our desires. We will have what we ask and find that we seek. If God sees that the birds are fed, He surely will not starve us. He will hear our call and will save us. He will hear and help us, if we fear Him, if we worship and serve Him with a holy awe of Him. Otherwise, how can we expect that He should accept us? (If we call upon Him in truth; for He desires truth in the inward part. We must be faithful to God, and sincere in our professions of dependence on Him, and devotedness to Him.

Day 244

God is a buckler to us who walk uprightly; who are sincere in their deportment before God and men; who walk according to the rule of the divine Word; who walk by faith on Christ, and go on

> **Proverbs 2:7 NIV**
>
> *He holds success in store for the upright, he is a shield to those whose walk is blameless.*

living by faith on His righteousness, which is walking in His uprightness, until they come to be with Him forever in heaven. To these the Lord is a "buckler" or shield; He covers them with the "shield of faith," His own Son, His blood righteousness, and sacrifice. No good thing has been withheld from us, and we have already been afforded all things necessary for life and godliness. God is our protector and our shield.

Day 245

Proverbs 11:25 NIV

A generous person will prosper; whoever refreshes others will be refreshed.

The liberal soul shall be made fat. The soul which blesses, not that merely prays for a blessing upon others, and wishes them well, and gives them good words, but bestows blessings on them, gives good things unto them liberally, cheerfully, and plentifully are blessed with temporal and spiritual blessings. They are in thriving and flourishing circumstances, both in soul and body. They who water will be watered also. They who largely share with others, like a flowing fountain of water, will have an abundance communicated to them again from God. Watering the plants in Christ's vineyard is one part of the work of a Gospel minister; "I have planted, Apollos watered" and such who do their work well are watered, rewarded, refreshed, and comforted of God.

Day 246

*W*hat works you do commit them unto the Lord, whether they are natural, civil, or religious. And in doing so, seek Him for strength and assistance in

> **Proverbs 16:3 ESV**
>
> *Commit your work to the LORD, and your plans will be established.*

all and leave the success of all with Him. Cast all your cares upon Him for supply, support, and sustain in life. Your thoughts will be established. When you have, by faith and in prayer, committed yourself, your case, your ways and works, to the Lord, your mind is made easy, your thoughts are composed and settled, and you quietly wait the issues of things. You say, "The will of the Lord is done." With confidence, you will know that God causes all things to work together for good. Whatever is for your good and God's glory shall be brought to pass. This knowledge will make you calm, sedate, and easy. This is the best way to have His designs, desires, and endeavors accomplished.

Day 247

Proverbs 17:17 NIV

A friend loves at all times, and a brother is born for a time of adversity.

Many times, we take our friends and their friendships for granted. Ideally, we see friends as people to share happy and exciting moments. **W**hen friendships go sour, we tend to quickly dissolve the friendships and move on. Proverbs 17:17 instructs us to love our friends at all times. And contrary to popular belief or opinion, friends are not solely for the purpose of good times. They are for times of adversity. Although God is our rock, our refuge, our strong tower and our salvation, He has permitted us to have fleshly beings that will assist in comforting us in times of trouble. So, if you have a friend or two, honor and cherish them.

Day 248

This verse describes God's sufficiency for the saints; His name is a strong tower for them, in which they may take rest when they are weary and take sanctuary

> **Proverbs 18:10 NIV**
>
> *The name of the LORD is a fortified tower; the righteous run to it and are safe.*

when they are pursued, where they may be lifted up above their enemies and fortified against them. There is enough in God to make us easy at all times. The wealth laid up in this tower is enough to enrich them, to be a continual feast and a continuing treasure to them. The strength of this tower is enough to protect them. The saints' security is in God. It is a strong tower to those who know how to make use of it as such. The righteous, by faith and prayer, devotion towards God and dependence on Him, run into it, as their city of refuge. Having made sure their interest in God's name, they take the comfort and benefit of it; they go out of themselves, retire from the world, live above, dwell in God and God in them, and so they are safe, they think themselves so, and they shall find themselves so.

Day 249

> **Isaiah 26:3 NIV**
>
> *You will keep in perfect peace those whose minds are steadfast, because they trust in you.*

When we trust in God, there are benefits. One such benefit is perfect peace. In Him, there is fullness of joy. When we focus on worldly events and the devastation going on around us, we have a tendency to become overwhelmed, overburdened, and even depressed. However, when we focus our attention on the Word of God, the decrees of God, the promises of God, the love of God, the faithfulness of God, the mercies of God, and the favors of God, we will find ourselves walking in the peace of God.

Day 250

*I*n ancient biblical times, God heard and answered the cries of His children. Because God is the same today as He was yesterday and the same as He will be tomorrow, He will continue to hear the cries of His children. So, when you need Him- cry out! He will hear you, and He will answer you. We are admonished in Philippians 4:6 to make our requests known unto the Lord.

> **Isaiah 30:19 NIV**
>
> *For the people shall dwell in Zion at Jerusalem: thou shalt weep no more: he will be very gracious unto thee at the voice of thy cry; when he shall hear it, he will answer thee.*

Day 251

Isaiah 41:13 KJV

For I the LORD thy God will hold thy right hand, saying unto thee, Fear not; I will help thee.

God will take hold of our right hand, creating an alliance with us and go hand in hand with us. As such, we need to fear no enemy. The alliance is expressive of great freedom, familiarity, and friendship, which should assure us of the strong affection God has towards us. In Him, we are safe. As the Lord holds our right hand, He is teaching us to walk by faith, leading us into His presence, to commune with Him. He keeps us from falling and will strengthen our right hand, so we will be able to do His work and service. He will relieve our wants and fill our hands with His good things. He will not leave us or forsake us (Adapted from Gill's Exposition of the Entire Bible).

Day 252

*W*aiting on the Lord is an act that demonstrates knowledge and reverence of God, confidence in Him, attendance on Him, not with the body only, in public and private, but with the soul also, and with some degree of constancy, and with patience and quietness. The Lord is to be waited upon for the manifestations of Him-

> **Isaiah 40:31 KJV**
>
> *But they that wait upon the LORD shall renew their strength; they shall mount up with wings as eagles; they shall run, and not be weary; and they shall walk, and not faint.*

self, who sometimes hides Himself, but is to be waited for. He has His set time to show Himself again, and His presence is worth waiting for. We should also wait for the performance of His promises, which were uttered from His throne. Remember, His Word will not return unto Him void, and in waiting, we are strengthened. We will be refreshed and reenergized. We will be able to press forward without tiredness. We will be upright and not faint. Be patient, and God will act.

Day 253

Isaiah 43:1 NLT

But now, O Jacob, listen to the LORD who created you. O Israel, the one who formed you says, "Do not be afraid, for I have ransomed you. I have called you by name; you are mine.

*T*hose whom He has redeemed by His precious blood are called by the grace of God to special blessings of grace, with a high, holy, and heavenly calling. They have no reason to fear anything, since they are the chosen of God. They have a right to all spiritual blessings; all things work together for their good; they shall persevere to the end, and at last be brought to glory, to which they are called. They are the Lord's. They voluntarily gave themselves to Him, under the influence of His Spirit and grace. They are His by profession and possession.

Day 254

*W*eapons formed against the people of God will fail to prosper. When tongues rise up in slander, they will fail. When fiery darts are aimed, they will fail. When blows are thrown, they will fail. Any weapon that rises up against the Word of God will be condemned and cast down. This is our inheritance in Christ Jesus, in whom we have righteous standing.

> **Isaiah 54:17 KJV**
>
> *No weapon that is formed against thee shall prosper; and every tongue that shall rise against thee in judgment thou shalt condemn. This is the heritage of the servants of the LORD, and their righteousness is of me, saith the LORD.*

Day 255

Isaiah 58:11 KJV

And the LORD shall guide thee continually, and satisfy thy soul in drought, and make fat thy bones: and thou shalt be like a watered garden, and like a spring of water, whose waters fail not.

God will direct us in all difficult and doubtful situations. The Lord will guide us continually. While we are here, in the wilderness of this world, we have need of continual direction from heaven. If at any time we are left to ourselves, we shall certainly miss our way. We are warned against being wise in our own eyes (Proverbs 3:7). The wisdom of God is our guide. Human wisdom fails, while God never fails.

Day 256

*T*hose who put their trust in God will find it is not in vain that they trust in Him. He is good to those who do so (Lam. 3:25). He is good

> **Lamentations 3:25 ESV**
>
> *The LORD is good to those who wait for him, to the soul who seeks him.*

to all, and all His creatures taste of His goodness. But there is a blessing of good for those that wait for Him, to the soul that seeks Him. When trouble is prolonged and deliverance is deferred, we must patiently wait for God. While we wait for Him by faith, we must seek Him by prayer: our souls must seek Him; otherwise, we will fail to find. Our seeking will help to keep up our waiting. The end result will be Him showing us marvelous loving kindness.

Day 257

Jeremiah 29:11 KJV

For I know the thoughts that I think toward you, saith the LORD, thoughts of peace, and not of evil, to give you an expected end.

Known unto God are all His works and all His thoughts. His works agree exactly with His thoughts. He does all according to the counsel of His will. But, we humans often do not know our own thoughts or our own mind, but God is never at any uncertainty within Himself. His thoughts are all working towards the expected end, which He will give in due time. He will give us an end, an expectation. He will give us to see the end of our troubles. Though it last long, it will not last always. As for God, His work is perfect. He will give us, not the expectations of our fears, nor the expectations of our fancies, but the expectations of our faith, the end which He has promised and which will turn for the best to us.

Day 258

The Lord is good to those that trust Him. To them, He will be a stronghold in the day of trouble. The same almighty power that is exerted for the terror and destruction of the wicked is engaged, and shall be

> **Nahum 1:7 NIV**
> *The LORD is good, a refuge in times of trouble. He cares for those who trust in him.*

employed, for the protection and satisfaction of His people. He is able both to save and to destroy. In the day of public trouble, when God's judgments are in the earth, laying all waste, He will be a place of defense to those that by faith put themselves under His protection, those that trust in Him in the way of their duty, that live a life of dependence upon Him, and devotedness to Him. He knows them; He takes them for His own. He takes cognizance of their case, knows what is best for them, and what course to take most effectually for their relief. They are perhaps obscure and little regarded in the world, but the Lord knows them.

Day 259

> **Proverbs 17:22 KJV**
>
> *A merry heart doeth good like a medicine: but a broken spirit drieth the bones.*

Stress, anxiety, and depression are death to our bodies. They kill us from the inside out. They are like a poison seeping from one part of us to another, like a cancer. However, when we are filled with joy, our heart is fulfilled. Joy, as an emotion, has the same power as debilitating emotions, but it has the opposite effect. Joy is like a medicine that cures us. It causes life to grow within us and purifies our innermost parts.

Day 260

There are many instructtions in these verses. We are told to ask, seek, and find. We must not only ask, but we must seek. We must second our prayers with our endeavors. Then, in asking and seeking, we must continue pressing, still knocking at the same door. We shall prevail, by our prayers, When we ask of God those things which Christ has here directed us to ask, that His name may be sanctified, that His kingdom may come, and His will be done, in these requests, we must be relentless and must never hold our peace day or night. We must not keep silent!

> **Luke 11:9-10 NIV**
>
> *So I say to you: Ask and it will be given to you; seek and you will find; knock and the door will be opened to you. For everyone who asks receives; the one who seeks finds; and to the one who knocks, the door will be opened.*

Day 261

John 3:16 KJV

For God so loved the world, that he gave his only begotten Son, that whosoever believeth in him should not perish, but have everlasting life.

*I*f we ever doubted how much God the Father loves us, His children, this scripture tells us plainly. He 'so' loved us, He gave to us His only begotten Son. He did not give us a counterfeit or any other type of replacement. He gave us His Son, the only begotten child of the King. And, if we believe in Christ, the son of God, we will not perish. Instead, we will have everlasting life. In Christ is the free gift of salvation, for no one can come to the Father except by the Son (John 14:6). He is our entry point.

Day 262

Verily, verily, I say unto you the words that proceed a particular truth, which can be depended upon. This particular truth is as follows: Those who believe in the Lord

> **John 6:47 JB 2000**
>
> *Verily, verily, I say unto you, He that believes in me has eternal life.*

Jesus Christ will have everlasting life. Not only may we have it, as in John 6:40, and will have it, but we have it already in Christ, our head and representative. We have it in the covenant of grace, and we have it in faith and hope. We have a right unto it as a fulfilled condition of our belief.

Now that the promise has been fulfilled, enjoy it! Celebrate it! Relish in it! Bask in it! Most importantly-share it!

Day 263

> **John 15:4 ESV**
>
> *Abide in me, and I in you. As the branch cannot bear fruit by itself, unless it abides in the vine, neither can you, unless you abide in me.*

Those that are come to Christ must abide in Him: "*Abide in me*, by faith; *and I in you*, by my Spirit; *abide in me*, and then fear not but I will *abide in you*." We must abide in Christ's word by regarding it. And with His Word in us, it is as a *light to our feet*. The knot of the branch abides in the vine, and the sap of the vine abides in the branch, and so there is a constant communication between them. The necessity of our abiding in Christ is to fulfill our fruitfulness. "*You cannot bring forth fruit, except you abide in me*; but, if you do, you *bring forth much fruit; for*, in short, *without me*, or separate from me, *you can do nothing*."

Day 264

Greater love has no man than this that a man lay down his life for his friends. The emphasis lies not on "friends," but on "laying down his life" for them. That is, one can

> **John 15:13 NIV**
>
> *Greater love has no one than this: to lay down one's life for one's friends.*

show no greater regard for those dear to him than to give his life for them. This is the love we will find in Christ.

Day 265

> ## Eph. 3:20-21 KJV
>
> *Now unto him that is able to do exceeding abundantly above all that we ask or think, according to the power that worketh in us. Unto him be glory in the church by Christ Jesus throughout all ages, world without end. Amen.*

*I*t is proper to conclude our prayers with praises, as Jesus has taught us to do. Take notice how He describes God, and how He ascribes glory to Him. He describes Him as a god that is able to do exceeding abundantly above all that we ask or think. Whatever we may ask or think to ask, God is still able to do more, abundantly more, exceeding abundantly more. In our applications to God, we should encourage our faith by a consideration of His all-sufficiency and almighty power: according to the power which works in us. The power that still works for the saints is according to that power that has been deposited in them. When we ask for grace from God, we ought to give glory to God. In ascribing glory to God, we ascribe all excellences and perfections to Him. The Mediator of these praises is Jesus Christ. All God's gifts come from Him to us through the hand of Christ; and all our praises pass from us to Him through the same hand.

Day 266

Philippians 4:8 KJV

Finally, brethren, whatsoever things are true, whatsoever things are honest, whatsoever things are just, whatsoever things are pure, whatsoever things are lovely, whatsoever things are of good report; if there be any virtue, and if there be any praise, think on these things.

---

*A*postle Paul places special emphasis on the breadth of the listed qualities by repeatedly using the indefinite adjective "whatever." He instructs believers to look for the true, noble, right, pure, lovely, admirable, excellent, and praiseworthy everywhere around us and to ponder the things in which these qualities are exemplified. When we are being persecuted by the society around us, we will be tempted to reject everything outside the church as indelibly tainted with evil. If so, then this list, with its admonition to look for the virtue in the wider world, reminds us, although society sometimes seems hostile and evil, it is still part of God's world and contains much good that the believer can affirm.

Day 267

*W*e live in a tempting world, where we are compassed about with snares. Every place, condition, relation, employment, and enjoyment, abounds with them. Yet, we can take comfort from this passage! God is faithful. Though Satan be a deceiver, God is true. He is wise as well as faithful, and will proportion our burden to our strength. He will not suffer us to be tempted above what we are able. He knows what we can bear, and what we can bear up against. He will take care that we be not overcome, if we rely upon Him, and resolve to approve ourselves faithful to Him. We need not perplex ourselves with the difficulties in our way when God will take care that they shall not be too great for us to encounter. He will make a way to escape. There is no valley so dark that He cannot find a way through it, no affliction so grievous that He cannot prevent, or remove, or enable us to support it, and in the end overrule it to our advantage.

> **I Cor. 10:13 NIV**
>
> *No temptation has overtaken you except what is common to mankind. And God is faithful; he will not let you be tempted beyond what you can bear. But when you are tempted, he will also provide a way out so that you can endure it.*

Day 268

Through our Lord Jesus Christ, God gives us the victory over sin the sting of death, over the law the strength of sin, and over death and the grave. He has the victory over sin; He has put it away by the sacrifice of

> **I Cor. 15:57 NIV**
>
> *But thanks be to God! He gives us the victory through our Lord Jesus Christ.*

Himself. He has finished and made an end of it. Christ has obtained a victory over the law. He has stopped its mouth and answered all its demands. He has been made under and subject to it. He has obeyed its precepts and bore its penalty and has delivered His people from the curse and condemnation of it, so they have nothing to fear from it. It is dead to them, and they to it. He has also abolished death by dying and rising again, so it shall have no more dominion over Him. And though they die, they shall not always remain under the power of death. They shall live again and with Him forever. He has conquered the grave by rising out of it Himself and from having the keys of the grave in His hands. He will at the last day oblige it to give up its dead (Adapted from John Gill's Exposition of the Entire Bible).

Day 269

> ### Luke 12:15 ISV
>
> *Then he told them, "Be careful to guard yourselves against every kind of greed, because a person's life doesn't consist of the amount of possessions he has."*

The Word of God clearly tells us that God will give us the desire of our hearts. There is no limit as to what God can and will provide unto His people. However, as believers, we are to take heed and beware of covetousness and the want of possessions for notoriety. Our lives do not consist of the abundance of the things which we possess. Our natural lives cannot be prolonged by all the good things of the world nor can they prevent diseases or death. Also, the comforts and happiness of life do not exist within these things. Our spiritual lives are not advantaged by our possessions and neither is our eternal life attained by the possession of worldly possessions. Let us focus on storing up treasures in heaven because earthly possessions and treasures are temporal.

Day 270

A believer's triumphs are all in Christ. In ourselves, we are weak, and have neither joy nor victory. But in Christ, we may rejoice and triumph. True believers have constant cause of triumph in Christ, for they are more than conquerors through Him who loves them.

II Cor. 2:14 WEB

Now thanks be to God, who always leads us in triumph in Christ, and reveals through us the sweet aroma of his knowledge in every place.

Day 271

> **II Cor. 4:8-9 NIV**
>
> *We are hard pressed on every side, but not crushed; perplexed, but not in despair; persecuted, but not abandoned; struck down, but not destroyed.*

*W*e as believers are afflicted many ways and are met with almost all sorts of troubles, yet not distressed. We are not hedged in because we can see help in God and receive help from God. We are often perplexed and not always without anxiety in our minds. Yet we are not in despair, even in our greatest perplexities, knowing God is able to support us and deliver us. In Him, we always place our trust and hope. We are persecuted by men, pursued with hatred and violence from place to place, as men not worthy to live, yet not forsaken of God. Believers may be sometimes forsaken of their friends, as well as persecuted by their enemies, but God will never leave them nor forsake them. We are sometimes dejected, or cast down, and our spirits begin to fail us. There may be fears within, yet we are not destroyed. Still, we were preserved, and our heads kept above water. Whatever condition the children of God may be in, in this world, they have a "but not" to comfort themselves with; their case sometimes is bad, yea very bad, but not so bad as it might be.

Day 272

Though the outside fleshly part of us will perish and decay, the inner man (our spirit) is regenerated daily by the Word of God. The afflictions we suffer are only momentary, but the eternal blessings are everlasting. We are to focus on that which is not seen rather what can be seen with our natural eyes. That which is material is temporal. We are to set our affections on the eternal.

> **II Cor. 4:16-18 NIV**
>
> *For which cause we faint not; but though our outward man perish, yet the inward man is renewed day by day. For our light affliction, which is but for a moment, worketh for us a far more exceeding and eternal weight of glory; While we look not at the things which are seen, but at the things which are not seen: for the things which are seen are temporal; but the things which are not seen are eternal.*

Day 273

> **II Cor. 5:7 KJV**
>
> *For we walk by faith, not by sight.*

*F*or we walk by faith, and not by sight. Faith is a grace which answers many useful purposes; it is the eye of the soul, by which it looks to Christ for righteousness, peace, pardon, life, and salvation; the hand by which receives Him and the foot which goes to Him and walks in Him as it has received Him. This denotes not a single act of faith, but a continued course of believing. It is expressive of a strong steady faith of glory and happiness. It is in opposition to "sight" and seeing with one's natural abilities (Adapted from John Gill's Exposition of the Entire Bible).

Day 274

Renewed men act upon new principles, by new rules, with new ends, and in new company. Believers are created anew; their hearts are not merely set right, but new hearts are given to them. They are the workmanship of God, created in Christ Jesus unto good works. The man who formerly saw no beauty in the

> **II Cor. 5:17 KJV**
>
> *Therefore if any man be in Christ, he is a new creature: old things are passed away; behold, all things are become new.*

Savior that he should desire Him, now loves Him above all things. The heart of the unregenerate is filled with enmity against God, and God is justly offended with him. Yet, there may be reconciliation. Our offended God has reconciled us to Himself by Jesus Christ. By the inspiration of God, the Scriptures were written, which are the word of reconciliation, showing that peace has been made by the cross, and how we may be interested therein (Adapted from Matthew Henry's Concise Commentary).

Day 275

Romans 8:6 KJV

For to be carnally minded is death; but to be spiritually minded is life and peace.

*W*hat we choose to focus on and then act on will determine whether we live or whether we die. Focusing on that which is worldly or fleshly will assuredly bring death either to our physical bodies, our spirits, or both. On the contrary, focusing on that which is of the Spirit will render life and peace. Deuteronomy 30:19 says, *"I call heaven and earth to record this day against you, that I have set before you life and death, blessing and cursing: therefore choose life, that both thou and thy seed may live."* Life is chosen by choosing that which is godly.

Day 276

*A*dhering to the conditions listed within this verse (loving God and being called according to His purpose) qualifies us to have all things work together for our good. Either directly or indirectly, every providence has a tendency toward the spiritual good of those that love God, breaking us off from sin, bringing us nearer to God, weaning us from the world, and fitting us for heaven.

> **Romans 8:28 KJV**
>
> *And we know that all things work together for good to them that love God, to them who are the called according to his purpose.*

Day 277

> **Romans 8:31 NIV**
>
> *What, then, shall we say in response to these things? If God is for us, who can be against us?*

The basis of the challenge is God's being for us. In this verse, Apostle Paul sums up all our privileges. This includes all God is for us. He performs all things for us. He is for us, even when He seems to act against us. And, if it is so, who can be against us, as to prevail against us, as to hinder our happiness? Even if they are so great and strong, ever so many, ever so malicious, what can they do? While God is for us, and we keep in His love, we may with a holy boldness defy all the powers of darkness. Let Satan do his worst. He is chained. Let the world do its worst, it is conquered. Principalities and powers are spoiled and disarmed, and triumphed over, in the cross of Christ. Who then dares fight against us, while God Himself is fighting for us?

Day 278

*A*postle Paul enumerates all those things which might attempt to separate Christ and believers; He concludes that it cannot be done. Neither the terrors of death on the one hand, nor the comforts and pleasures of life on the other, neither the fear of death nor the hope of life. Both the good angels and the bad are called principalities and powers. The good angels will not, the bad shall not, and neither can. The good angels are engaged friends; the bad are restrained enemies.

Neither the sense of troubles present nor the fear of troubles to come. Time shall not separate us, eternity shall not. Nor any other creature. It will not, it cannot, separate us

> **Romans 8:38-39 NIV**
>
> *For I am convinced that neither death nor life, neither angels nor demons, neither the present nor the future, nor any powers, neither height nor depth, nor anything else in all creation, will be able to separate us from the love of God that is in Christ Jesus our Lord.*

from the love of God, which is in Christ Jesus our Lord. It cannot cut off or impair our love to God, or God's to us. The love that exists between God and true believers is through Christ (Adapted from Matthew Henry's Commentary).

Day 279

That which is written of Christ, concerning His self-denial and sufferings, is written for our learning; He left us an example. If Christ denied Himself, surely, we should deny ourselves, from a principle of ingenuousness and of gratitude, and especially of conformity to His image. The example of Christ, in what He did and said, is recorded for our imitation.

That which is written in the scriptures of the Old Testament in general is written for our learning. What happened to the Old Testament saints happened to them for example; and the scriptures of the Old Testament have many fulfilling. The scriptures are left for a standing rule to us: they were written that they might remain for our use and benefit.

> **Romans 15:4 KJV**
>
> *For whatsoever things were written aforetime were written for our learning, that we through patience and comfort of the scriptures might have hope.*

Day 280

Christ is said to dwell in His people, as He is always present with them by His gracious influences and operations. It is desirable to have Christ dwell in our hearts. If the law of Christ is written there, and the love of Christ be shed abroad there, then Christ dwells there. Faith opens the door of the soul, to receive Christ. Faith admits Him and submits to Him. By faith, we are united to Christ and have an interest in Him. By the breadth of it, we may understand the extent of it to all ages, nations, and ranks of men.

> **Ephesians 3:17-19 NIV**
>
> *So that Christ may dwell in your hearts through faith. And I pray that you, being rooted and established in love, may have power, together with all the Lord's holy people, to grasp how wide and long and high and deep is the love of Christ, and to know this love that surpasses knowledge—that you may be filled to the measure of all the fullness of God.*

By the length of it, it continues from everlasting to everlasting. By the depth of it, it stooping to the lowest condition, with a design to relieve and save those who have sunk into the depths of sin and misery.

Day 281

Mark 12:30-31 NIV

Love the Lord your God with all your heart and with all your soul and with all your mind and with all your strength.' The second is this: 'Love your neighbor as yourself.' There is no commandment greater than these."

The Lord our God is one Lord. If we firmly believe this, then we shall love Him with all our heart. He is Jehovah, who has all amiable perfections in Himself; He is our God, to whom we stand related and obliged; therefore, we ought to love Him, to set our affections on Him, and take delight in Him. If He is one Lord, our hearts must be one with Him, and since there is no God besides, no rival must be admitted with Him upon the throne. The second great commandment is to love our neighbor as ourselves, as truly and sincerely as we love ourselves, and in the same instances, and we must show it by doing unto others as we would like done unto us. Our neighbor and we are of one body, of one society, that of the world of mankind. For a fellow-Christian, of the same sacred society, the obligation is even stronger.

Day 282

Satan, our adversary, is constantly seeking whom he can devour. Without our defenses about us, we will easily become his prey. We are to put on the helmet of salvation and the breastplate of righteousness, have the sword of the spirit in our hand, gird our loins about with truth, carry the shield of faith, and have our feet shod with the preparation of the gospel of peace. This is the full armor of God. We must be fully equipped for the spiritual battle the enemy wants to entangle us in. Remember, the Bible says in Ephesians 6:12, *"For we wrestle not against flesh and blood, but against principalities, against powers, against the rulers of the darkness of this world, against spiritual wickedness in high places."*

Ephesians 6:10-11 KJV

Finally, my brethren, be strong in the Lord, and in the power of his might. Put on the whole armour of God, that ye may be able to stand against the wiles of the devil.

Day 283

> ### Phil. 3:7-9 KJV
>
> *But what things were gain to me, those I counted loss for Christ. Yea doubtless, and I count all things but loss for the excellency of the knowledge of Christ Jesus my Lord: for whom I have suffered the loss of all things, and do count them but dung, that I may win Christ, And be found in him, not having mine own righteousness, which is of the law, but that which is through the faith of Christ, the righteousness which is of God by faith.*

*H*e counted the things that were gain to him as lost for Christ. They were not only insufficient to enrich him, but what would certainly impoverish and ruin him, if he trusted in them, in opposition to Christ. He tells us what he was ambitious of and reached after: it was the knowledge of Christ Jesus his Lord. It was not a merely notional and speculative, but a practical and efficacious knowledge of Him. We are undone without a righteousness wherein to appear before God, for we are guilty. There is a righteousness provided for us in Jesus Christ, and it is a complete and perfect righteousness.

Day 284

Philippians 4:4-7 KJV

Rejoice in the Lord alway: and again I say, Rejoice. Let your moderation be known unto all men. The Lord is at hand. Be careful for nothing; but in every thing by prayer and supplication with thanksgiving let your requests be made known unto God. And the peace of God, which passeth all understanding, shall keep your hearts and minds through Christ Jesus.

---

*I*t is commonplace in our modern society to be locked into time schedules and faced with meeting deadlines. With these obligations, we have a tendency to become anxious. However, we are advised in Phil. 4:4-7, it is better to do all things in moderation and with prayer and supplication. *W*hen life becomes overwhelming, we are to go to God and make our requests known. He will give us the peace we need as we endure the trials of life. This peace we will not be able to understand; however, it will keep our hearts and minds through Jesus Christ.

Day 285

Philippians 4:19 KJV
But my God shall supply all your need according to his riches in glory by Christ Jesus.

When we obey the commandments of the Lord, He is obligated by His own words to bless us. All our needs will be supplied when we are obedient to what God has told us to do. God is not a man that He should lie. Whatsoever He promises will be done. But, we must first do what we have been commanded, and then God will perform His Word with signs following.

Day 286

We are called to be at peace with God as our privilege and peace with our brethren as our duty.

Colossians 3:15 KJV

And let the peace of God rule in your hearts.

Being united in one body, we are called to be at peace one with another, as the members of the natural body, for *we are the body of Christ, and members in particular* (1 Cor. 12:27). Instead of envying one another upon account of any particular favors and excellence, we are to be thankful for His mercies, which are common to all of us. And be careful not to complain. We are to use our mouths to praise the Lord and to thank Him for His goodness. We often times are quick to complain rather than to give praise and thanks. But, we have the ability to turn that situation around- today!

Day 287

II Thessalonians 3:3 ESV

But the Lord is faithful. He will establish you and guard you against the evil one.

God is able to establish you: in the doctrines of the Gospel, so as not to be moved away from them, or to be finally and totally seduced by those unreasonable and wicked men. He will keep you from evil: from the evil of sin; not from the being and commission of it entirely, which is not to be expected in this life, but from the dominion of it. He will guard you from the evil one Satan, from his snares and temptations, so as to be entangled and overcome by them. God is faithful, who will not suffer you to be tempted beyond your strength, but will enable you to bear it, and make a way for your escape, and deliver out of it. Likewise, He will deliver you from evil men, unreasonable and wicked men, so as not to be drawn aside by them, by their principles and practices, by their frowns or flatteries. All in all, God is our deliverer.

Day 288

The spirit of fear comes to grip our hearts and immobilize us. God did not intend for us to be subjected to this demonic influence. II Timothy 1:7

> **II Timothy 1:7 KJV**
>
> *For God hath not given us the spirit of fear; but of power, and of love, and of a sound mind.*

clearly states, God equipped us with power, love and a sound mind. We must use the power we have to extinguish the fiery darts of the enemy, one being the dart of fear. The only type of fear we should have in our lives is the fear of the Lord God. This fear is reverence for the only true living God.

Day 289

> **II Timothy 4:18 NIV**
>
> *The Lord will rescue me from every evil attack and will bring me safely to his heavenly kingdom. To him be glory for ever and ever. Amen.*

As the Lord stands by us, He strengthens us, in times of difficulty and danger and His presence more than satisfies every one's absence. When the Lord preserves His servants from great and imminent danger, it is for eminent work and service. He has a purpose for us, and it is imperative that the purpose is fulfilled. For example, Paul was preserved so that by him the preaching might be fully known, etc. Former deliverances should encourage future hopes. There is a heavenly kingdom, to which the Lord will preserve His faithful witnessing or suffering servants. We ought to give God the glory of all past, present, and future deliverances:

Day 290

*D*uring the time Christ spent here on earth, He was not exempt from temptations, sufferings, evildoers and the like. He experienced much of that which we do today. After coming out of the wilderness from a 40-day fast, Jesus was

> **Hebrews 2:18 NIV**
> *Because he himself suffered when he was tempted, he is able to help those who are being tempted.*

tempted of the devil. He was given the choice to serve Satan in exchange for all the kingdoms of the world. He was tempted by Satan to use His majestic powers to turn stones into bread to satisfy His physical hunger. In all of Satan's temptations, Jesus resisted him and Satan fled. What are you being tempted to do that is contrary to the Word of God? What is going on in your life that has you in a state of desperation that is giving you pause to think about devious methods to cure what is ailing you? Use the Word of God and pull down every vain imagination that is trying to exalt itself against the Word of God. Let the Word work for you and shut the mouth of the enemy.

Day 291

> **Hebrews 3:6 KJV**
>
> *But Christ as a son over his own house; whose house are we, if we hold fast the confidence and the rejoicing of the hope firm unto the end.*

The Jews had a high opinion of the faithfulness of Moses, yet his faithfulness was but a type of Christ's. Christ was the Master of the house, of His church, His people, as well as their Maker. Moses was a faithful servant; Christ, as the eternal Son of God, is the rightful owner and sovereign ruler of the church. There must not only be setting out well in the ways of Christ, but steadfastness and perseverance therein to the end. Every meditation on His person and His salvation will suggest more wisdom, new motives to love, confidence, and obedience.

Day 292

*T*he 'Word of God,' whether the verse is referring to Jesus (John 1:1) or the Word itself, is *quick*. It is very lively and active, in all its efforts, in seizing the conscience of sinners, in cutting them to the heart, and in comforting them and binding up the

> **Hebrews 4:12 KJV 2000**
>
> *For the word of God is living and powerful! It is sharper than any two-edged sword, piercing to the dividing of soul and spirit, and of the joints and marrow, and is a discerner of the thoughts and intentions of the heart.*

wounds of the soul. Those who call the Word of God a dead letter or an outdated book do not fully know it or understand it. Saints die, and sinners die, but the Word of God lives. Matthew 5:18 states, not one jot or tittle of God's Word will pass away, even if heaven and earth do.

Day 293

> **II Peter 1:3 KJV**
>
> *According as his divine power hath given unto us all things that pertain unto life and godliness, through the knowledge of him that hath called us to glory and virtue.*

Life can be likened to a bed of roses. It is filled with sweet fragrances and indescribable beauty. At the same time, there are prickly obstacles that often come to test our faith and may even cause us to question God's involvement in our life. II Peter 1:3 tells us, God has provided for us all things we need for this life and godliness, including diligence, virtue, knowledge, temperance, patience, brotherly kindness, and love (v. 5-7).

Day 294

*W*hether we experience times of joy or times of pain, our Lord and Savior Jesus Christ will be with us every step of the way. When He departed this earthly realm, He said He must go, but He would send another comforter: the Holy Spirit. The Holy Spirit is our guide. He keeps us on the straight and narrow path. He comforts us. He teaches us. He speaks to us. He is our present help in our times of trouble. He will never leave or forsake us.

> **Hebrews 13:5 KJV**
>
> *Let your conversation be without covetousness; and be content with such things as ye have: for he hath said, I will never leave thee, nor forsake thee.*

Day 295

James 1:2-4 KJV
My brethren, count it all joy when ye fall into divers temptations; Knowing this, that the trying of your faith worketh patience. But let patience have her perfect work, that ye may be perfect and entire, wanting nothing.

Our trials may be of many and different kinds. Therefore, we have need to put on the whole armor of God. We must be armed on every side, because temptations lie on all sides. We must not sink into a sad and disconsolate frame of mind, which would make us faint under our trials. We must endeavor to keep our spirits dilated and enlarged. The trying of one's grace produces another; and the more the suffering graces of a Christian are exercised, the stronger they grow. After we have abounded in other graces, we have need of patience (Heb. 10:36). But let patience have its perfect work, and we shall be perfect and entire, wanting nothing.

Day 296

Every soul that truly loves God, shall have its trials in this world. The commands of God, and the dealings of His providence try men's hearts and show the dispositions which prevail in them. But nothing sinful in the heart or conduct can be ascribed to God. He is not the author of the impure matter, though His fiery trial exposes it. Afflictions, as sent by God, are designed to draw out our graces, but not our corruptions. The origin of

> **James 1:12-15 KJV**
> *Blessed is the man that endureth temptation: for when he is tried, he shall receive the crown of life, which the Lord hath promised to them that love him. Let no man say when he is tempted, I am tempted of God: for God cannot be tempted with evil, neither tempteth he any man: But every man is tempted, when he is drawn away of his own lust, and enticed. Then when lust hath conceived, it bringeth forth sin: and sin, when it is finished, bringeth forth death.*

evil and temptation is in our own hearts. Stop the beginnings of sin, or all the evils that follow must be wholly charged upon us. God has no pleasure in the death of men, as He has no hand in their sin.

Day 297

Submit your understanding to the truth of God; submit your wills to the will of His precepts, the will of His providence. Submit yourselves to God, for He is ready to do you good. If we yield to temptations, the devil will continually follow us, but if we put on the whole armor of God, and stand out against him, he will leave us. Let sinners then submit to God and seek His grace and favor, resisting the devil. All sin must be wept over, here in godly sorrow, or hereafter, in eternal misery. And the Lord will not refuse to comfort one who really mourns for sin, or to exalt one who humbles himself before Him.

> **James 4:7-8 NIV**
>
> *Submit yourselves, then, to God. Resist the devil, and he will flee from you. Come near to God and he will come near to you. Wash your hands, you sinners, and purify your hearts, you double-minded.*

Day 298

*W*e cast our anxiety upon God when we fulfill the Lord's commandment, by taking no thought to what will we eat or what will we drink or with what shall we be clothed. For our

> **1 Peter 5:7 NLT**
> *Give all your worries and cares to God, for he cares about you.*

heavenly Father knows we have need of all these things. God cares for us; therefore, we must not be over-anxious, but trust in Him. He knows we have need of all these things, and He makes all things work together for good to His chosen, to them that love Him.

Day 299

> **1 John 4:4 NIV**
>
> *You, dear children, are from God and have overcome them, because the one who is in you is greater than the one who is in the world.*

*W*e are born of God, taught of God, anointed of God, and secured against infectious fatal delusions. God has His chosen, who shall not be mortally seduced. He gives them hope of victory.

*W*e have overcome the deceivers and their temptations, and there is good ground of hope that we will do so still. The Spirit of God dwells in you, and that Spirit is mightier than men of devils. It is a great happiness to be under the influence of the Holy Ghost. The Spirit of God has framed our minds for God and heaven.

Day 300

*W*hen love prevails, fear ceases. We must distinguish between fear and being afraid. Or, in this case, between the fear of God and being afraid of Him. The fear of God is often mentioned and commanded as the substance of religion (1 Pet. 2:17; Rev. 14:7); and so, it imports the high regard and

> **I John 4:18 KJV**
>
> *There is no fear in love; but perfect love casteth out fear: because fear hath torment. He that feareth is not made perfect in love.*

veneration we have for God and His authority and government. Such fear is constant with love. But then there is being afraid of God, which arises from a sense of guilt and a view of His vindictive perfections; in the view of them, God is represented as a consuming fire. So, fear here may be rendered dread. There is no dread in love. Love considers its object as good and excellent, and therefore amiable and worthy to be beloved. Love considers God as most eminently good and most eminently loving us in Christ, and so puts off dread, and puts on joy in Him; and, as love grows, joy grows too; so that perfect love casts out fear or dread.

Day 301

> **I John 5:14-15 NIV**
>
> *This is the confidence we have in approaching God: that if we ask anything according to his will, he hears us. And if we know that he hears us—whatever we ask—we know that we have what we asked of him.*

The Lord Christ emboldens us to come to God in all circumstances, with all our supplications and requests. Through Him our petitions are admitted and accepted of God. The matter of our prayer must be agreeable to the declared will of God. It is not fit that we should ask what is contrary either to His majesty and glory or to our own good, who are His and dependent on Him. And then, we may have confidence that the prayer of faith shall be heard in heaven. Great are the deliverances, mercies, and blessings, which the holy petitioner needs. To know that his petitions are heard or accepted is as good as to know that they are answered; and, therefore, that he is so pitied, pardoned, or counseled, sanctified, assisted, and saved (or shall be so) as he is allowed to ask of God.

Day 302

*T*hat which has required their patience, and about which it has been exercised, what they have been patiently waiting for, namely, the destruction of antichrist; and now it will be come, and patience will have its perfect work. And the faith of Jesus,

> **Revelation 14:12 NIV**
>
> *This calls for patient endurance on the part of the people of God who keep his commands and remain faithful to Jesus.*

meaning either the grace of faith, of which Jesus is the object, author, and finisher; and which these saints will have from Him, and exercise upon Him in a very strong and comfortable manner; and which, and the profession of it, they will hold fast to the end; or else the doctrine of faith, concerning the person, office, and grace of Jesus Christ, the faith once delivered to the saints, which they will have contended for, stood fast in, and now will hold in a pure conscience.

Day 303

Romans 15:13 NIV

May the God of hope fill you with all joy and peace in believing, so that by the power of the Holy Spirit you may abound in hope.

May the God of this hope - that God who caused both Jews and Gentiles to hope that the gracious promises which He made to them should be fulfilled; and who, accordingly, has fulfilled them in the most punctual and circumstantial manner, fill you with all joy - Give you true spiritual happiness; peace in your own hearts, and unity among yourselves; in believing not only the promises which He has given you, but believing in Christ Jesus, in whom all the promises are yea and amen. That ye may abound in hope - That ye may be excited to take more enlarged views of the salvation which God has provided for you, and have all your expectations fulfilled by the power of the Holy Ghost, enabling you to hope and believe; and then sealing the fulfillment of the promises upon your hearts.

Day 304

*W*e should love the Lord, our Strength, and our Salvation; we should call on Him in every trouble, and praise Him for every deliverance. We should aim to walk with Him in all righteousness and true holiness, keeping from sin. If we belong to Him, He conquers and reigns for us, and we shall conquer and reign through Him, and partake of the mercy of our anointed King, which is promised to all His seed for evermore.

> **Psalm 18:32-34 NIV**
>
> *The God who equipped me with strength and made my way blameless. He made my feet like the feet of a deer and set me secure on the heights. He trains my hands for war, so that my arms can bend a bow of bronze.*

Day 305

I Cor. 2:7-9 KJV

But we speak the wisdom of God in a mystery, even the hidden wisdom, which God ordained before the world unto our glory: Which none of the princes of this world knew: for had they known it, they would not have crucified the Lord of glory. But as it is written, Eye hath not seen, nor ear heard, neither have entered into the heart of man, the things which God hath prepared for them that love him.

Those who receive the doctrine of Christ as divine and having been enlightened by the Holy Spirit, see not only the plain history of Christ and Him crucified, but the deep and admirable designs of divine wisdom therein. It is the mystery made manifest to the saints (Col 1:26), though formerly hidden from the heathen world. It was only shown in dark types and distant prophecies, but now is revealed and made known by the Spirit of God. Jesus Christ is the Lord of glory. There are many things, which people would not do, if they knew the wisdom of God in the great work of redemption. There are things God hath prepared for those that love Him, and wait for Him. We must take them as they stand in the Scriptures, as God hath been pleased to reveal them to us.

Day 306

Death is a great loss to a carnal, worldly man, for he loses all his earthly comforts and all his hopes. But to a true believer it is gain, for it is the end of all his weakness and misery. It delivers him from all the evils of life and brings him to possess the chief good. The apostle's difficulty was

> **Philippians 1:21-23 NIV**
>
> *For to me to live is Christ, and to die is gain. If I am to live in the flesh, that means fruitful labor for me. Yet which I shall choose I cannot tell. I am hard pressed between the two. My desire is to depart and be with Christ, for that is far better.*

not between living in this world and living in heaven; between these two there is no comparison but between serving Christ in this world and enjoying Him in another. Not between two evil things, but between two good things; living to Christ and being with Him. See the power of faith and of Divine grace; it can make us willing to die. In this world, we are compassed with sin; but when with Christ, we shall escape sin and temptation, sorrow and death, forever. But those who have most reason to desire to depart should be willing to remain in the world as long as God has any work for them to do. And the more unexpected mercies are before they come, the more of God will be seen in them.

Day 307

*J*esus is not here, for He has ascended. We expect His second coming thence, to gather in all the citizens of that New Jerusalem to Himself. At the second coming of Christ, we expect to be happy and glorified there. There is good reason to have our conversation in heaven, not only because Christ is now there, but because we hope to be there shortly. He shall change our vile bodies, that they may be fashioned like unto His glorious body (Phil. 3:21). There is a glory reserved for the bodies of the saints, which they will be instated in at the resurrection. The body is now at the best a vile body- the body of our humiliation; it has its rise and origin from the earth; it is supported out of the earth and is subject to many diseases and to death at last. But this all soon will change.

> **Philippians 3:20-21 NIV**
>
> *But our citizenship is in heaven, and from it we await a Savior, the Lord Jesus Christ, who will transform our lowly body to be like his glorious body, by the power that enables him even to subject all things to himself.*

Day 308

*A*postle Paul shares words of encourage-ment to ancient-day believers that is yet applicable to modern-day believers. It is imperative that we know who we are in Christ Jesus. Like Paul, we should be fully persuaded that no matter what force may come against us: death (the crucifixion of Christ), life (with

> **Romans 8:37-39 KJV**
>
> *Nay, in all these things we are more than conquerors through him that loved us. For I am persuaded, that neither death, nor life, nor angels, nor principalities, nor powers, nor things present, nor things to come, Nor height, nor depth, nor any other creature, shall be able to separate us from the love of God, which is in Christ Jesus our Lord.*

its afflictions/trials), angels (good or evil), principalities/powers (not even those with the highest rank), not our past nor our future, height nor depth (mountains, barriers, the great abyss), or creatures (nothing beneath the Almighty God), we will not be separated from God's love.

Day 309

> **I John 4:7-8 NIV**
>
> *Beloved, let us love one another, for love is from God, and whoever loves has been born of God and knows God. Anyone who does not love does not know God, because God is love.*

The Spirit of God is the Spirit of love. He that does not love the image of God in his people, has no saving knowledge of God. For it is God's nature to be kind and to give happiness. The law of God is love; and all would have been perfectly happy, had all obeyed it. The provision of the gospel, for the forgiveness of sin, and the salvation of sinners, consistently with God's glory and justice, shows that God is love. Mystery and darkness rest upon many things yet. God has so shown Himself to be love, that we cannot come short of eternal happiness, unless through unbelief and impenitence, although strict justice would condemn us to hopeless misery, because we break our Creator's laws. None of our words or thoughts can do justice to the free, astonishing love of a holy God towards sinners, who could not profit or harm Him, whom He might justly crush in a moment, and whose deserving of His vengeance was shown in the method by which they were saved, though He could by His almighty Word have created other worlds, with more perfect beings, if He had seen fit (Matthew Henry's Commentary).

Day 310

The Lord is God in the highest realms and among celestial beings. His throne is set in glory, above all, out of reach of foes, in the place of universal oversight. He who

> **Psalm 136:26 KJV**
>
> *O give thanks unto the God of heaven: for his mercy endureth for ever.*

feeds ravens and sparrows is yet the glorious God of the highest realms. Angels count it their glory to proclaim his glory in every heavenly street. See herein the greatness of His nature, the depth of His condescension, and the range of His love. Mark the one sole cause of His bounty - "For his mercy endureth for ever." He hath done all things from this motive; and because His mercy never ceases, He will continue to multiply deeds of love world without end. Let us with all our powers of heart and tongue give thanks unto the holy name of Jehovah for ever and ever (The Treasury of David).

Day 311

> **Galatians 2:20 KJV**
>
> *I am crucified with Christ: nevertheless I live; yet not I, but Christ liveth in me: and the life which I now live in the flesh I live by the faith of the Son of God, who loved me, and gave himself for me.*

*T*o believe in Christ crucified is not only to believe that He was crucified, but also to believe that we are crucified with Him. And this is to know Christ crucified.

*H*ence, we learn the nature of grace. God's grace cannot stand with man's merit. Grace is no grace unless it is freely given every way. The more simply we rely on Christ for everything, the more devotedly do we walk before Him in all His ordinances and commandments. Christ lives and reigns in us, and we live here on earth by faith in the Son of God, which works by love, causes obedience, and changes into His holy image. Thus, He neither abuses the grace of God, nor makes it in vain.

Day 312

Joshua 1:7-9 NIV

Only be strong and very courageous, being careful to do according to all the law that Moses my servant commanded you. Do not turn from it to the right hand or to the left, that you may have good success wherever you go. This Book of the Law shall not depart from your mouth, but you shall meditate on it day and night, so that you may be careful to do according to all that is written in it. For then you will make your way prosperous, and then you will have good success. Have I not commanded you? Be strong and courageous. Do not be frightened, and do not be dismayed, for the LORD your God is with you wherever you go.

---

*L*ike Joshua, we are to make the law of God our rule. We are charged to meditate therein day and night, that we might understand it. Whatever affairs of this world we have in mind, we must not neglect the one thing needful. We must ourselves be under command; no man's dignity or dominion sets him above the law of God. We are to encourage ourselves with the promise and presence of God. When we are in the way of duty, we have reason to be strong and very bold. Our Lord Jesus was borne up under His sufferings by a regard to the will of God and the commandment from His Father. And so shall it be with us.

Day 313

Psalm 27:1 KJV

The LORD is my light and my salvation; whom shall I fear? the LORD is the strength of my life; of whom shall I be afraid?

*G*od is a light to His people, to show them the way when they are in doubt, to comfort and rejoice their hearts when they are in sorrow. It is in His light that they now walk on in their way, and in His light, they hope to see light forever. God, who is a believer's light, is the strength of his life, not only by whom, but in whom, he lives and moves. In God, therefore, let us strengthen ourselves (Matthew Henry's Commentary).

Day 314

God's elect were sinners in Adam; hence, they were polluted and guilty. So, they are in their own persons while unregenerated: they are dead in sin, and live in it, commit it, are slaves unto it, and are

> **Romans 5:8 ESV**
>
> *But God shows his love for us in that while we were still sinners, Christ died for us.*

under the power and dominion of it; and many of them are the chief and vilest of sinners. This is what they were considered when Christ died for them. But are not God's people sinners after conversion? Yes, but sin does not have dominion over them. Their lives are not a course of sinning, as before. They are openly justified and pardoned, as well as renewed, and sanctified, and live in newness of life. This illustrates the love of God to them, notwithstanding their character and condition.

Day 315

I John 3:1 NIV
See what kind of love the Father has given to us, that we should be called children of God; and so we are. The reason why the world does not know us is that it did not know him.

*L*ittle does the world know of the happiness of the real followers of Christ. Little does the world think that these poor, humble, despised ones are favorites of God and will dwell in heaven.

*L*et the followers of Christ be content with hard fare here, since they are in a land of strangers, where their Lord was so badly treated before them. The sons of God must walk by faith and live by hope. They may well wait in faith, hope, and earnest desire, for the revelation of the Lord Jesus. The sons of God will be known and be made manifest by likeness to their Head. They shall be transformed into the same image, by their view of Him.

Day 316

*C*hristians must avoid useless expense and be careful not to contract any debts they have not the power to discharge. They are also to stand aloof from all venturesome speculations, rash engagements, and whatever may expose them to the danger of not rendering to all their due. Do not keep in any one's debt. Give everyone his/her own. Do not spend that on yourselves which you owe to others. But many who are very sensible of the trouble, think little of the sin of being in debt. The last five of the Ten Commandments

> **Romans 13:8 ESV**
>
> *Owe no one anything, except to love each other, for the one who loves another has fulfilled the law.*

are all summed up in this royal law: Thou shalt love thy neighbor as thyself, with the same sincerity that thou loves thyself, though not in the same measure and degree. He that loves his neighbor as himself will desire the welfare of his neighbor. On this is built that golden rule, of doing as we would be done by. Love is a living, active principle of obedience to the whole law.

Day 317

The gospel is a doctrine according to godliness and is so far from giving the least countenance to sin that it lays us under the strongest obligation to avoid and subdue it. Apostle Paul urges that all the law is fulfilled in one word, even in this: Thou shall love thy neighbor as thyself. If Christians would help one another and rejoice with one another, the quarrelling can be diminished. Happy would it be, if Christians, instead of biting and devouring one another on account of different opinions, would set themselves against sin in themselves, and in the places where they live.

> **Galatians 5:13 NASB**
>
> *For you were called to freedom, brethren; only do not turn your freedom into an opportunity for the flesh, but through love serve one another.*

Day 318

*W*e are to understand humility, which is opposed to pride. Patience implies bearing injuries, without seeking revenge. Christians have need to bear one with another, to make the best one of another, to provoke one another's graces and not their passions. Without these things unity cannot be preserved. The first step towards unity is humility; without this there will be no meekness, no patience, or forbearance; and without these no unity. Pride and passion break the peace, and make all the mischief. Humility and meekness restore the peace and keep it. Only by pride comes contention; only by humility comes love. The more lowly-mindedness, the more like-mindedness. We do not walk worthy of the vocation wherewith we are called if we are not meek and lowly of heart.

> **Ephesians 4:2 NIV**
>
> *Be completely humble and gentle; be patient, bearing with one another in love.*

Day 319

> **I Peter 1:22 NIV**
>
> *Now that you have purified yourselves by obeying the truth so that you have sincere love for each other, love one another deeply, from the heart.*

The Spirit of God is the great agent in the purification of man's soul. The Spirit convinces the soul of its impurities, furnishes those virtues and graces that both adorn and purify, such as faith, hope, the fear of God, and the love of Jesus Christ. The Spirit excites our endeavors and makes them successful. The aid of the Spirit does not supersede our own industry; these people purified their own souls, but it was through the Spirit. The souls of Christians must be purified before they can so much as love one another without interference. There are such lusts and partialities in man's nature that without divine grace we can neither love God nor one another as we ought to do; there is no charity but out of a pure heart. It is the duty of all Christians sincerely and fervently to love one another. Our affection to one another must be sincere and real, and it must be fervent, constant, and extensive.

Day 320

The Lord Jesus teaches that we must show all the real kindness we can to all, especially to the souls of others. We must pray for them. While many will render good for good, we must render good for evil; and this will speak a nobler principle than most men act

> **Matt. 5:43-44 NKJV**
>
> *You have heard that it was said, 'You shall love your neighbor and hate your enemy.' But I say to you, Love your enemies and pray for those who persecute you.*

by. Others salute their brethren and embrace those of like kind, but we must not so confine our respect. It is the duty of Christians to desire, aim at, and press towards perfection in grace and holiness. And therein, we must study to conform ourselves to the example of our heavenly Father (1Pe 1:15-16). Surely, more is to be expected from the followers of Christ than from others; surely more will be found in them than in others. Let us implore God to enable us to prove ourselves His children.

Day 321

When attempting to serve two masters, it is impossible to serve them both equally. The service to one will outweigh the service to the other. We should strive to be single minded in our service. Many attempt to serve God and strive for material gain. Many times, the desire for more and more material wealth causes an extreme shortage of the praise and worship that is given to God.

> **Matthew 6:24-25 NIV**
>
> *No one can serve two masters. Either you will hate the one and love the other, or you will be devoted to the one and despise the other. You cannot serve both God and money.*

Day 322

*L*ove is the leading affection of the soul; the love of God is the leading grace in the renewed soul. Where this is not, nothing else that is good is done, or done right, or accepted, or done long. Loving God with all our heart will effectually take us off from and arm us against all those things that are rivals with Him for the throne in our souls, and will engage us to every-thing by which He may be honored and with which He will be pleased.

> **Mark 12:28-30 KJV**
>
> *And one of the scribes came, and having heard them reasoning together, and perceiving that he had answered them well, asked him, Which is the first commandment of all? And Jesus answered him, The first of all the commandments is, Hear, O Israel; The Lord our God is one Lord: And thou shalt love the Lord thy God with all thy heart, and with all thy soul, and with all thy mind, and with all thy strength: this is the first commandment.*

Day 323

John 14:21-24 NASB

He who has My commandments and keeps them is the one who loves Me; and he who loves Me will be loved by My Father, and I will love him and will disclose Myself to him.

Having Christ's commands, we must keep them. And having them in our heads, we must keep them in our hearts and lives. The surest evidence of our love to Christ is obedience to the laws of Christ. There are spiritual tokens of Christ and His love given to all believers. Where sincere love to Christ is in the heart, there will be obedience. Love will be a commanding, constraining principle. And where love is duty follows from a principle of gratitude. God will not only love obedient believers, but He will take pleasure in loving them and will rest in love to them. These privileges are confined to those whose faith works by love and whose love to Jesus leads them to keep His commandments. Such are partakers of the Holy Spirit's new-creating grace.

Day 324

Those whom God loves as a Father may despise the hatred of all the world. As the Father loved Christ, who was most worthy, so He loved His disciples, who were unworthy. All that love the Savior should continue in their love to Him and take all occasions to show it. The joy of the hypocrite is but for a moment, but the joy of those who abide in Christ's love is

> **John 15:9-10 NIV**
>
> *As the Father has loved me, so have I loved you. Abide in my love. If you keep my commandments, you will abide in my love, just as I have kept my Father's commandments and abide in his love.*

a continual feast. They are to show their love to Him by keeping His commandments. If the same power that first shed abroad the love of Christ's in our hearts did not keep us in that love, we should not long abide in it. Christ's love to us should direct us to love each other (Matthew Henry's Concise Commentary).

Day 325

Jude 1:21 KJV

Keep yourselves in the love of God, looking for the mercy of our Lord Jesus Christ unto eternal life.

*K*eep yourselves in the love of God, the love by which God loves His people. We are exhorted to keep ourselves in it, to set it always before us, to keep it constantly in view, to exercise faith on it, firmly believing our interest in it. We must also meditate on it, give ourselves up wholly to the contemplation of it, and employ our thoughts constantly about it, which is the foundation of all grace here and glory hereafter. We are to preserve ourselves by it, against Satan's temptations, the snares of the world, and the lusts of the flesh. Whenever Satan solicits us to sin and any snare is laid to draw into it and the flesh attempts to be predominant, we should take ourselves to the love of God and preserve ourselves from sin. It would not be wise to depend on anything that can be done by men; nor is there any danger of real believers falling from it, or losing it, since it is unchangeable, and is from everlasting to everlasting; or else by the love of God we are to understand that love with which His people love Him and of which He is the object (Luke 11:42) (Adapted from John Gill's Exposition of the Entire Bible).

Day 326

*T*rue religion, consisting in the fear of the Lord, which is the wisdom before recom-mended, teaches men to hate all sin, as it is displeasing to God and destructive to the soul. The fear of the Lord is to hate evil, the evil way, to hate sin as sin, and therefore to hate every false way.

> **Proverbs 8:13 KJV**
>
> *The fear of the LORD is to hate evil: pride, and arrogancy, and the evil way, and the froward mouth, do I hate.*

*W*herever there is an awe of God, there is a dread of sin, as an evil, as only evil, particularly to hate pride and passion, those two common and dangerous sins. Conceitedness of ourselves, pride and arrogancy, are sins which Christ hates, and so do all those who have the Spirit of Christ. Everyone hates them in others, but we must hate them in ourselves. The froward mouth, peevishness towards others, God hates, because it is such an enemy to the peace of mankind, and therefore, we should hate it. Be it spoken to the honor of religion that however it is unjustly accused, it is so far from making men conceited and sour that there is nothing more directly contrary to it than pride and passion, nor which it teaches us more to detest.

Day 327

Romans 12:3 NIV

For by the grace given me I say to every one of you: Do not think of yourself more highly than you ought, but rather think of yourself with sober judgment, in accordance with the measure of faith God has given you.

Apostle Paul warns us about walking in the proper perspective about who we are. It is one thing to have pride about who God has made you to be. This is the sense of having a healthy self-esteem and walking in the assurance of Christ. However, being prideful (thinking more of yourself than you should) will only lead to destruction. Likewise, when we walk in self-doubt, we face the same challenge. When we have an improper self-concept, we will undoubtedly end up on the wrong path in life. Apostle Paul tells us, we must know who we are and not think more highly or lower of ourselves than who we actually are.

Day 328

*A*s we walk through our lives, we should be sure to seek guidance from those who are wise. Many have walked where we are trying to go. They can offer us pearls of wisdom to keep us from making shipwrecks.

> **Proverbs 11:14 KJV**
>
> *Where no counsel is, the people fall: but in the multitude of counselors there is safety.*

*W*here no counsel is, but everything done rashly, or no prudent consultation for the common good, but only caballing for parties and divided interests, the people fall, crumble into factions, fall to pieces, fall together by the ears, and fall an easy prey to their common enemies. Councils of war are necessary to the operations of war; two eyes see more than one; and mutual advice is in order to mutual assistance. In the multitude of counselors, that see their need one of another, and act in concert and with concern for the public welfare, there is safety. In our private affairs, we shall often find it to our advantage to obtain advice with many. If they agree in their advice, our way will be the clearer. If they differ, we shall hear what is to be said on all sides and be better able to determine.

Day 329

> **II Corinthians 2:11 KJV**
>
> *Lest Satan should get an advantage of us: for we are not ignorant of his devices.*

Satan is a subtle enemy and uses many strategies to deceive us, and we should not be ignorant of his devices. He is also a watchful adversary, who is ready to take all advantages against us, and we should be very cautious lest we give him any occasion to do it. Satan, under pretense of showing a just indignation against sin and keeping up a strict and righteous discipline, destroys souls, ruins churches, and brings religion into contempt. This was one of his devices in former times, that persons who fell into any gross sin after baptism and a profession of religion, were never to be restored and received into the communion of the church again, let their repentance be ever so sincere. This cruel and inexorable spirit, under the show of strict religion and discipline, is what Apostle Paul here would caution against, as one of the wiles of Satan.

Day 330

*I*n the midst of trials, do not fear. God is with you. He knows your every trial and your every weakness. He is your strength. Lean on His everlasting arms. Allow Him to undergird you. He will hold you up in times of weakness. Fear not, dear heart.

> **Isaiah 41:10 NIV**
>
> *So do not fear, for I am with you; do not be dismayed, for I am your God. I will strengthen you and help you; I will uphold you with my righteous right hand.*

Day 331

Philippians 4:19 KJV

But my God shall supply all your need according to his riches in glory by Christ Jesus.

When we obey the commandments of the Lord, He is obligated by His own words to bless you. All your needs will be supplied when we are obedient to what God has told us to do. God is not a man that He should lie. Whatsoever He promises will be done. But, we must first do what we have been commanded and then God will perform His Word with signs following.

Day 332

"The love of Christ" does not mean the saints' love to Christ, but His love to them; Apostle Paul is speaking not of our love to Christ, but of the love of God and Christ to us, not tribulation or affliction; or distress (whether of body

> **Romans 8:35 KJV**
>
> *Who shall separate us from the love of Christ? shall tribulation, or distress, or persecution, or famine, or nakedness, or peril, or sword?*

or mind) or persecution (from the world, for this is rather an evidence that Christ has loved us, chosen and called us, because the world hates us); or famine (want of the necessities of life, as food and drink); or nakedness (desire of adequate clothing)or peril (dangers); or sword (death by the sword or any other weapon) shall separate us from His love.

Day 333

> **Hebrews 11:1-3 KJV**
>
> *Now faith is the substance of things hoped for, the evidence of things not seen. For by it the elders obtained a good report. Through faith we understand that the worlds were framed by the word of God, so that things which are seen were not made of things which do appear.*

Faith always has been the mark of God's servants, from the beginning of the world. Where the principle is planted by the regenerating Spirit of God, it will cause the truth to be received, concerning justification by the sufferings and merits of Christ. And the same things that are the object of our hope are the objects of our faith. It is a firm persuasion and expectation that God will perform all He has promised to us in Christ. This persuasion allows the soul to enjoy those things now; it allows them to maintain that reality in the soul, by the first-fruits and foretastes of them. Faith affirms to the mind the reality of things that cannot be seen by the bodily eye. It is a full approval of all God has revealed as holy, just, and good.

Day 334

Through our Lord Jesus Christ, God gives us the victory over sin (the sting of death), over the law (the strength of sin), and over death and the grave. He has the victory over sin; He has put it away by the sacrifice of

> **I Cor. 15:57 NIV**
>
> *But thanks be to God! He gives us the victory through our Lord Jesus Christ.*

Himself. He has finished and made an end of it. Christ has obtained a victory over the law. He has stopped its mouth and answered all its demands. He has been made under and subject to it. He has obeyed its precepts and bore its penalty and has delivered His people from the curse and condemnation of it, so that they have nothing to fear from it. It is dead to them, and they to it. He has also abolished death by dying and rising again, so it shall have no more dominion over Him. And though they die, they shall not always remain under the power of death. They shall live again and with Him forever. He has conquered the grave by rising out of it Himself and from having the keys of the grave in His hands. He will at the last day oblige it to give up its dead (Adapted from John Gill's Exposition of the Entire Bible).

Day 335

*I*t is proper to conclude our prayers with praises, as Jesus has taught us to do. Take notice how He describes God and how He ascribes glory to Him. He describes Him as a god that is able to do exceeding abundantly above all that we ask or think. Whatever we may ask or think to ask, God is still able to do more, abundantly more, exceeding abundantly more. In our applications to God, we should encourage our faith by a consideration of His all-sufficiency and almighty power: according to the power which works in us. The power that still works for the saints is according to that power that has been deposited in them. When we ask for grace from God, we ought to give glory to God. In ascribing glory to God, we ascribe all excellences

> **Eph. 3:20-21 KJV**
>
> *Now unto him that is able to do exceeding abundantly above all that we ask or think, according to the power that worketh in us. Unto him be glory in the church by Christ Jesus throughout all ages, world without end. Amen.*

and perfections to Him. The Mediator of these praises is Jesus Christ. All God's gifts come from Him to us through the hand of Christ; and all our praises pass from us to Him through the same hand.

Day 336

*A*postle Paul shares words of encouragement to ancient-day believers that is yet applicable to modern-day believers. It is imperative that we know who we are in Christ Jesus. Like Paul, we should be fully per-suaded that no matter what force may come against us: death (the crucifixion of Christ), life (with its afflictions/trials),

> **Romans 8:37-39 KJV**
>
> *Nay, in all these things we are more than conquerors through him that loved us. For I am persuaded, that neither death, nor life, nor angels, nor principalities, nor powers, nor things present, nor things to come, Nor height, nor depth, nor any other*

angels (good or evil), principalities/powers (not even those with the highest rank), not our past nor our future, height nor depth (mountains, barriers, the great abyss), or creatures (nothing beneath the Almighty God), we will not be separated from God's love.

Day 337

Psalm 118:14-16 KJV

The LORD is my strength and song, and is become my salvation. The voice of rejoicing and salvation is in the tabernacles of the righteous: the right hand of the LORD doeth valiantly. The right hand of the LORD is exalted: the right hand of the LORD doeth valiantly.

The Lord is my strength and my song; that is, I make Him so (without Him I am weak and sad, but in Him, I stay myself as my strength, both for doing and suffering, and in Him, I solace myself as my song, by which I both express my joy and ease my grief), and making Him so, I find Him so. He strengthens my heart with His graces and gladdens my heart with His comforts. If God be our strength, He must be our song; if He works all our works in us, He must have all praise and glory from us. God is sometimes the strength of His people when He is not their song; they have spiritual supports when they want spiritual delights. But, if He is both to us, we have abundant reason to triumph in Him; for, He is our strength and our song, He has become not only our Savior, but our salvation; for His as our strength is our protection to the salvation, and His as our song is an earnest and foretaste of the salvation (Matthew Henry Commentary).

Day 338

*G*od's promises are found in His Word. We have a promise in Hebrews 13:5, where God tells us He will never leave us nor forsake us. In Luke 20:43, He promises He will make our

Psalm 119: 50 NIV

My comfort in my suffering is this: Your promise preserves my life.

enemies our footstool. Daniel 12:2 promises us everlasting life after an earthly death. In the abundance of His Word are an abundance of promises. There, we shall find comfort.

Day 339

Colossians 3:15 KJV
And let the peace of God rule in your hearts.

*W*e are called to this peace, to peace with God as our privilege and peace with our brethren as our duty. Being united in one body, we are called to be at peace one with another, as the members of the natural body; for we are the body of Christ and members in particular (I Cor. 12:27). To preserve in us this peaceable disposition, we must be thankful. The work of thanksgiving to God is such a sweet and pleasant work that it will help to make us sweet and pleasant towards all men. Instead of envying one another upon account of any particular favors and excellence, be thankful for His mercies, which are common to all of you. And be careful not to complain. Use your mouth to praise the Lord and to thank Him for His goodness. We often times are quick to complain rather than to give praise and thanks.

Day 340

*P*ride will have a fall. Those that are of a haughty spirit, that think of themselves above what is meet and look with contempt

> **Proverbs 16:18 NIV**
>
> *Pride goes before destruction, a haughty spirit before a fall.*

upon others, that with their pride affront God and disquiet others, will be brought down, either by repentance or by ruin. It is the honor of God to humble the proud (Job 40:11-12). It is the act of justice that those who have lifted up themselves should be laid low. Pharaoh, Sennacherib, and Nebuchadnezzar were instances of this. Men cannot punish pride, but either admire it or fear it. Therefore, God will take the punishing of it into His own hands. He alone will deal with proud men. Proud men are frequently most proud, and insolent, and haughty, just before their destruction. When proud men set God's judgments at defiance and think themselves at the greatest distance from them, it is a sign that they are at the door. Therefore, let us not fear the pride of others, but greatly fear pride in ourselves.

Day 341

> **Psalm 92:14 KJV**
>
> *They shall still bring forth fruit in old age; they shall be fat and flourishing.*

The products of sanctification, all the instances of a lively devotion and a useful conversation, good works, by which God is glorified and others are edified are the fruits of righteousness, in which it is the privilege, as well as the duty, of the righteous to abound. Their abounding in them is the matter of a promise as well as of a command. It is promised that they shall bring forth fruit in old age. Other trees, when they are old, leave off bearing, but in God's trees, the strength of grace does not fail with the strength of nature. The last days of the saints are sometimes their best days, and their last work is their best work. This indeed shows that they are upright; perseverance is the surest evidence of sincerity.

Day 342

*M*oses assures Israel of the constant presence of God with them. This is applied to all God's spiritual Israel, to encourage their faith and hope; unto us is this gospel preached, as

> **Deuteronomy 31:8 NIV**
>
> *The LORD himself goes before you and will be with you; he will never leave you nor forsake you. Do not be afraid; do not be discouraged.*

well as unto them; He will never fail thee, nor forsake thee. Moses commends Joshua to them for a leader; one whose wisdom, and courage, and affection they had long known; one whom God had appointed to be their leader, and therefore would own and bless. Joshua is well pleased to be admonished by Moses to be strong and of good courage. Those shall speed well, who have God with them; therefore, they ought to be of good courage. Through God let us do valiantly, for through Him, we shall do victoriously; if we resist the devil, he will flee from us.

Day 343

> **Proverbs 18:10 NIV**
>
> *The name of the LORD is a fortified tower; the righteous run to it and are safe.*

This verse describes God's sufficiency for the saints; His name is a strong tower for them, in which they may take rest when they are weary and take sanctuary when they are pursued, where they may be lifted up above their enemies and fortified against them. There is enough in God to keep us at ease at all times. The wealth laid up in this tower is enough to enrich them, to be a continual feast and a continuing treasure to them. The strength of this tower is enough to protect them. The saints' security is in God. It is a strong tower to those who know how to make use of it as such. The righteous, by faith and prayer, devotion towards God and dependence on Him, run into it, as their city of refuge. Having made sure their interest in God's name, they take the comfort and benefit of it; they go out of themselves, retire from the world, live above, dwell in God and God in them, and so they are safe, they think themselves so, and they shall find themselves so.

Day 344

Romans 13:7 says to give to those what is due them. In Romans 16:3-4, Apostle Paul is honoring Priscilla and Aquila for the service they have rendered unto him and unto other believers. To whom is honor due in your life? Don't withhold the honor; be gracious and obedient to

> **Romans 16:3-4 KJV**
>
> *Greet Priscilla and Aquila my helpers in Christ Jesus: Who have for my life laid down their own necks: unto whom not only I give thanks, but also all the churches of the Gentiles.*

God's Word and issue the honor that is due. Encourage, love, and respect are great tools for edifying the body of Christ.

Day 345

> **Revelation 12:11 KJV**
>
> *And they overcame him by the blood of the Lamb, and by the word of their testimony; and they loved not their lives unto the death.*

The servants of God overcame Satan, by the blood of the Lamb. Christ, by dying, destroyed the devil that had the power of death. By the word of their testimony, as the great instrument of war, the sword of the Spirit, which is the Word of God, by a resolute powerful preaching of the everlasting gospel, which is mighty, through God, to pull down strongholds, and by their courage and patience in sufferings; they loved not their lives unto the death, when the love of life stood in competition with their loyalty to Christ; they loved not their lives so well but they could give them up to death, could lay them down in Christ's cause; their love to their own lives was overcome by stronger affections of another nature; and this their courage and zeal helped to confound their enemies, to convince many of the spectators, to confirm the souls of the faithful, and so contributed greatly to this victory.

Day 346

There is no greater enemy to Christian love than pride and passion. If we do things in contradiction to our brethren, this is doing them through strife. If we do them through ostentation of ourselves, this is doing them through vainglory:

> **Philippians 2:3 NKJV**
> *Let nothing **be done** through selfish ambition or conceit, but in lowliness of mind let each esteem others better than himself.*

both are destructive of Christian love and kindle unchristian contentions. Christ came to slay all enmities; therefore, let there not be among Christians a spirit of opposition. Christ came to humble us, and therefore let there not be among us a spirit of pride. We must esteem others in lowliness of mind better than ourselves, be severe upon our own faults and charitable in our judgments of others, be quick in observing our own defects and infirmities, but ready to overlook and make favorable allowances for the defects of others. We must esteem the good, which is in others above that which is in ourselves, for we best know our own unworthiness and imperfections. We must interest ourselves in the concerns of others, not in a way of curiosity and censoriousness, or as busybodies in other men's matters, but in Christian love and sympathy.

Day 347

> **I Corinthians 15:4-6 NIV**
>
> *Christ was buried, that he was raised on the third day according to the Scriptures, and that he appeared to Cephas, and then to the Twelve. After that, he appeared to more than five hundred of the brothers and sisters at the same time, most of whom are still living, though some have fallen asleep.*

The doctrine of Christ's death and resurrection is the foundation of Christianity. Remove this and all our hopes for eternity sink at once. And it is by holding this truth firm that Christians stand in the day of trial and are kept faithful to God. We believe in vain, unless we keep in the faith of the gospel. This truth is confirmed by Old Testament prophecies; many saw Christ after He was risen. When sinners are, by divine grace, turned into saints, God causes the remembrance of former sins to make them humble, diligent, and faithful. True believers, though not ignorant of what the Lord has done for, in, and by them, yet when they look at their whole conduct and their obligations, they are led to feel that none are so worthless as they are. All true Christians believe that Jesus Christ, and Him crucified, and then risen from the dead, is the sum and substance of Christianity.

Day 348

The Lord our God is one Lord. If we firmly believe this, then we shall love Him with all our heart. He is Jehovah, who has all amiable perfections in Himself; He is our God, to whom we stand related and obliged; therefore, we ought to love Him, to set our affections on Him, and take delight in Him. If He is one Lord, our hearts must be one with Him, and since there is no God besides, no rival

> **Mark 12:30-31 NIV**
>
> *Love the Lord your God with all your heart and with all your soul and with all your mind and with all your strength.' The second is this: 'Love your neighbor as yourself.' There is no commandment greater than these."*

must be admitted with Him upon the throne. The second great commandment is to love our neighbor as ourselves, as truly and sincerely as we love ourselves, and in the same instances, and we must show it by doing unto others as we would like done unto us. Our neighbor and we are of one body, of one society, that of the world of mankind. For a fellow-Christian, of the same sacred society, the obligation is even stronger.

Day 349

> **Exodus 15:26 ESV**
>
> *"If you will diligently listen to the voice of the LORD your God, and do that which is right in his eyes, and give ear to his commandments and keep all his statutes, I will put none of the diseases on you that I put on the Egyptians, for I am the LORD, your healer."*

But in every trial we should cast our care upon the Lord, and pour out our hearts before him. We shall then find that a submissive will, a peaceful conscience, and the comforts of the Holy Ghost, will render the bitterest trial tolerable, yea, pleasant. Moses did what the people had neglected to do; he cried unto the Lord.

And God provided graciously for them. He directed Moses to a tree which he cast into the waters, when, at once, they were made sweet. Some make this tree typical of the cross of Christ, which sweetens the bitter waters of affliction to all the faithful, and enables them to rejoice in tribulation. But a rebellious Israelite shall fare no better than a rebellious Egyptian. The threatening is implied only, the promise is expressed. God is the great Physician. If we are kept well, it is he that keeps us; if we are made well, it is he that recovers us. He is our life and the length of our days. Let us not forget that we are kept from destruction, and delivered from our enemies, to be the Lord's servants.

Day 350

*K*eep yourselves in the love of God, the love by which God loves His people. We are exhorted to keep ourselves in it, to set it always before us, to keep it constantly in view, to exercise faith on it, firmly believing our interest in it. We

> **Jude 1:21 KJV**
>
> *Keep yourselves in the love of God, looking for the mercy of our Lord Jesus Christ unto eternal life.*

must also meditate on it, give ourselves up wholly to the contemplation of it, and employ our thoughts constantly about it, which is the foundation of all grace here and glory hereafter. We are to preserve ourselves by it, against Satan's temptations, the snares of the world, and the lusts of the flesh. Whenever Satan solicits us to sin and any snare is laid to draw into it and the flesh attempts to be predominant, we should take ourselves to the love of God and preserve ourselves from sin. It would not be wise to depend on anything that can be done by men; nor is there any danger of real believers falling from it, or losing it, since it is unchangeable, and is from everlasting to everlasting; or else by the love of God we are to understand that love with which His people love Him and of which He is the object (Luke 11:42). (Adapted from John Gill's Exposition of the Entire Bible).

Day 351

> **2 Timothy 3:16-17 KJV**
>
> *All scripture is given by inspiration of God, and is profitable for doctrine, for reproof, for correction, for instruction in righteousness that the man of God may be perfect, thoroughly furnished unto all good works.*

All scripture is divine revelation, which we may depend upon as infallibly true. The same Spirit that breathed reason into us breathes revelation among us. The prophets and apostles did not speak from themselves, but that which they received of the Lord that they delivered unto us. The Word of God is a sure guide in our way to eternal life. The scriptures are able to make us truly wise, wise for our souls and another world. It is profitable to us for all the purposes of the Christian life, for doctrine, for reproof, for correction, for instruction in righteousness. It answers all the ends of divine revelation. It instructs us in that which is true, reproves us for that which is amiss, and directs us in that which is good. It is of use to all, for we all need to be instructed, corrected, and reproved: it is of special use to ministers, who are to give instruction, correction, and reproof. Mankind is perfected by the Word of God in this world by scripture. By it, we are thoroughly furnished for every good work.

Day 352

There are three interpretations for this verse, and all are applicable to the King of glory. First, it refers to the ascension of Christ into heaven, and the welcome given to Him there. Our Redeemer

> **Psalm 24:7 KJV**
>
> *Lift up your heads, O ye gates; and be ye lift up, ye everlasting doors; and the King of glory shall come in.*

found the gates of heaven shut, but having by His blood made atonement for sin, as one having authority, He demanded entrance. Second, it can refer to Christ's entrance into the souls of men by His Word and Spirit, that they may be His temples. Behold, He stands at the door, and knocks (Revelation 3:20). The gates and doors of the heart are to be opened to Him, as possession is delivered to the rightful owner. Third, it also may refer to His second coming with glorious power. Lord, open the everlasting door of our souls by thy grace, that we may now receive thee, and be completely yours, and that, at length, we may be numbered with your saints in glory.

Day 353

> **Ephesians 6:12 NKJV**
>
> *For we do not wrestle against flesh and blood, but against principalities, against powers, against the rulers of the darkness of this age, against spiritual hosts of wickedness in the heavenly places.*

*W*hen we encounter problems with other persons, from our humanness, we want to fight fire with fire. More appropriately, we want to fight flesh with flesh. If someone hurts us with words, we want to return the favor with words. However, when we begin to understand that it is not truly the person who is attacking us, but a spirit that is operating through the person, we will not retaliate in kind. Instead, we will war according to scripture. Ephesians 6:12 tells us that our fight is not against flesh and blood, but against principalities, powers, rulers of darkness, and spiritual wickedness. Therefore, the battle must continue to be fought in the spirit. It begins in the spirit and must be fought in the spirit, so it can be conquered in the spirit. The weapons of our warfare are not carnal, but mighty through God for the pulling down of strongholds (II Cor. 10:4).

Day 354

When no one else will, nor can, nor dare to shelter me, the Lord is my defense, to preserve me from the evil of my troubles, from sinking under them and being ruined by them. He is the rock of my refuge, in the clefts of which I may take shelter, and on the top of which I may set my feet, to be out of the reach of danger. God is His people's refuge, to whom they may flee, in whom they are safe and may be secure. He is the rock of their refuge, so strong, so firm, impregnable, immovable, as a rock.

> **Psalm 94:22 KJV**
>
> *But the LORD is my defence; and my God is the rock of my refuge.*

Day 355

Luke 6:38 KJV

Give, and it shall be given unto you; good measure, pressed down, and shaken together, and running over, shall men give into your bosom. For with the same measure that ye mete withal it shall be measured to you again.

*W*hen the instruction to *give* has been properly responded to, God is obligated to fulfill the second part of the verse. Your action prompts God's reaction. God's reaction is the blessing flow. He would not have you give and not make sure you are a receiver as well. God is giving back to you, He presses the gift down, so He will have room to add more. While God is giving you a good portion and pressing it down to add more, He also shakes the gift. Shaking permits the uneven pieces the opportunity to fit together better, resulting in less unused spaces in the receptacle. At this point, the receptacle used to house God's blessing is now full. There is no more room for any more to fit. However, God does not cease His giving. He continues to pour out until the gift is running over, thus providing us with more than enough for ourselves as well as enough to give others. The gifts that God blesses us with are not *only* for us. They are meant to be shared.

Day 356

There is no greater enemy to Christian love than pride and passion. If we do things in contradiction to our brethren, this is doing them through strife. If we do them through ostentation of ourselves, this is doing them through vain-glory: both are

> **Philippians 2:3 NKJV**
>
> *Let nothing **be done** through selfish ambition or conceit, but in lowliness of mind let each esteem others better than himself.*

destructive of Christian love and kindle unchristian contentions. Christ came to slay all enmities; therefore, let there not be among Christians a spirit of opposition. Christ came to humble us, and therefore let there not be among us a spirit of pride. We must esteem others in lowliness of mind better than ourselves, be severe upon our own faults and charitable in our judgments of others, be quick in observing our own defects and infirmities, but ready to overlook and make favorable allowances for the defects of others. We must esteem the good, which is in others above that which is in ourselves, for we best know our own unworthiness and imperfections. We must interest ourselves in the concerns of others, not in a way of curiosity and censoriousness, or as busybodies in other men's matters, but in Christian love and sympathy.

Day 357

> **Hebrews 10:23 KJV**
>
> *Let us hold fast the profession of our faith without wavering; (for he is faithful that promised).*

*F*or God (Father, Son, and Spirit) is faithful that promised. God the Father is a promising God and is known to be so by His people; He is eminently and emphatically the Promiser. The promises of God are exceeding great and precious, very ancient, free, and unconditional, irrevocable and immutable, and are admirably suited to the cases of His people and will be fulfilled- every one of them. His promises include in them things temporal, spiritual, and eternal. God is faithful to all His promises, nor can He fail or deceive. He is all wise and foreknowing of everything that comes to pass. He never changes His mind nor forgets His Word. He is able to perform His Word. He is the God of truth and cannot lie; nor has He ever failed in anyone of His promises, nor will He suffer His faithfulness to fail; and this is a strong argument to hold fast a profession of faith.

Day 358

II Corin. 12:9-10 KJV

And he said unto me, My grace is sufficient for thee: for my strength is made perfect in weakness. Most gladly therefore will I rather glory in my infirmities, that the power of Christ may rest upon me. Therefore I take pleasure in infirmities, in reproaches, in necessities, in persecutions, in distresses for Christ's sake: for when I am weak, then am I strong.

---

*J*esus was persecuted for spreading the gospel of the good news. As believers, we know that we will suffer persecution for the sake of the gospel also. Even in our persecution, God will not forsake us. In this, we can we can find solace.

*T*he stress of life can weaken our endurance, but in Christ we are strengthened. Thus, we are fortified to endure personal attacks, character assassinations, distresses, backbiting, slander, reproach, jealousy, envy, strife, etc. Although attacks of this nature can be emotionally devastating, God's grace is sufficient for us to endure all.

Day 359

Romans 14:16 NIV

Do not allow what you consider good to be spoken of as evil.

Be careful about doing anything that may give occasion to others to speak evil, either of the Christian religion in general, or of your Christian liberty in particular. The gospel is your good; the liberties and franchises, the privileges and immunities, granted by it are your good; your knowledge and strength of grace to discern and use your liberty in things disputed are your good, a good which the weak brother has not. Now, let not this be evil spoken of. It is true we cannot hinder loose and ungoverned tongues from speaking evil of us and of the best things we have; but we must not (if we can help it) give them any occasion to do it. Let not the reproach arise from any default of ours, meaning do not make yourself despicable. For example, do not use your knowledge and strength in such a manner as to give occasion to people to call it presumption, loose walking, and disobedience to God's law. We must deny ourselves in many cases for the preservation of our credit and reputation, forbearing to do that which we rightly know we may lawfully do, when our doing it may be a prejudice to our good name, especially when it has the appearance of evil.

Day 360

The Lord our God is one Lord. If we firmly believe this, then we shall love Him with all our heart. He is Jehovah, who has all amiable perfections in Himself; He is our God, to whom we stand related and obliged; therefore, we ought to love Him, to set our affections on Him, and take delight in Him. If He is one Lord, our hearts must be one with Him, and since there

> **Mark 12:30-31 NIV**
>
> *Love the Lord your God with all your heart and with all your soul and with all your mind and with all your strength.' The second is this: 'Love your neighbor as yourself.' There is no commandment greater than these."*

is no God besides, no rival must be admitted with Him upon the throne. The second great commandment is to love our neighbor as ourselves, as truly and sincerely as we love ourselves, and in the same instances, and we must show it by doing unto others as we would like done unto us. Our neighbor and we are of one body, of one society, that of the world of mankind. For a fellow-Christian, of the same sacred society, the obligation is even stronger.

Day 361

Philippians 4:13 KJV

I can do all things through Christ which strengtheneth me.

*W*e as humans are incapable of doing everything we need to do with our limited human strength, whether it is physical strength, emotional strength, psychological strength, etc. But in Christ, we are supplied with the appropriate measure of strength we need to accomplish those tasks that seem to present a challenge for us. In Him, there isn't any task too difficult that we are unable to accomplish. We must always remember- In Him, we live; in Him, we move; and, in Him, we have our being!

*H*ave faith in who God has called you to be. Many doubt the very gifts and talents that God has placed in them to use to fulfill a specific task. They ask themselves if they can fulfill their heart's burning desires. If God called you to do something, He will give you what is needed to fulfill the task.

Day 362

*W*e often question why things happen to us, and we sometimes fail to see the necessity of certain events in our lives. But we must be wise enough to acknowledge nothing happens to us without God knowing about it. Therefore, if God allows it to occur, there must be a reason. These are opportunities to exercise our faith in God. We must lean not to our own understanding, but hold fast to Romans 8:28-31 that clearly tells us that each event works together. Our life is not lived as isolated events. They fit together as one giant puzzle and some-thing good is coming out of it- if you allow God's will to be done in your life.

> **Romans 8:28-31 KJV**
>
> *And we know that all things work together for good to them that love God, to them who are the called according to his purpose. For whom he did foreknow, he also did predestinate to be conformed to the image of his Son, that he might be the firstborn among many brethren. Moreover whom he did predestinate, them he also called: and whom he called, them he also justified: and whom he justified, them he also glorified. What shall we then say to these things? If God be for us, who can be against us?*

Day 363

> **Psalm 32:8 NIV**
>
> *I will instruct you and teach you in the way you should go; I will counsel you with my loving eye on you.*

*S*ome apply this to God's conduct and direction. He teaches us by His Word and guides us with His eye, by the secret intimations of His will in the hints and turns of Providence, which He enables His people to understand and take direction from, as a master makes a servant know his mind by a wink of his eye. When Christ turned and looked upon Peter, He guided him with His eye. But it is rather to be taken as David's promise to those who sat under his instruction, his own children and family especially: *"I will counsel thee; my eye shall be upon thee." "I will give thee the best counsel I can and then observe whether thou takest it or no."* Those that are taught in the Word should be under the constant inspection of those that teach them; spiritual guides must be overseers. In this application of the foregoing doctrine concerning the blessedness of those whose sins are pardoned, we have a word to sinners and a word to saints; and this is rightly dividing the Word of truth and giving to each his/her portion (Matthew Henry's Commentary).

Day 364

"O taste and see." Make a trial, an inward, experimental trial of the goodness of God. You cannot see except by tasting for yourself; but if you taste you shall see, for this, like Jonathan's honey, enlightens

> **Psalm 34:8 NIV**
>
> *Taste and see that the LORD is good; blessed is the one who takes refuge in him.*

the eyes. *"That the Lord is good."* You can only know this really and personally by experience. There is the banquet with its oxen and fatlings; its fat things full of marrow, and wines on the lees well refined; but their sweetness will be all unknown to you except you make the blessings of grace your own, by a living, inward, vital participation in them. *"Blessed is the man that trusteth in him."* Faith is the soul's taste; they who test the Lord by their confidence always find Him good, and they become themselves blessed. The second clause of the verse is the argument in support of the exhortation contained in the first sentence (The Treasury of David).

Day 365

> **Psalm 30:6-7 NIV**
>
> *When I felt secure, I said, "I will never be shaken." LORD, when you favored me, you made my royal mountain stand firm; but when you hid your face, I was dismayed.*

David, like many of us, was blinded by his prosperity, the blessings he received from the Lord. He was highly favored of God and began to pay more attention to his material wealth than to the praise and worship of the one who poured out the blessings. When God hid His face from David, David knew He had fallen short and disappointed God. Are you like David? Have you begun to glorify and worship material gains rather than the one who blessed you with them? We must be steadfast and unmovable in our worship of God. He should be our focus at all times, for God is the one who gives us the power to get wealth and not we ourselves (Deuteronomy 8:18).

Gift of Salvation for Non-Believers

*"For all have sinned, and come short of the
glory of God."*
Romans 3:23

This section was written especially for non-believers, those who have not accepted the gift of salvation. The gift of salvation saves souls from eternal damnation and is a free gift offered by God Himself. John 3:16-18 says, "*For God so loved the world, that he gave his only begotten Son, that whosoever believeth in him should not perish, but have everlasting life. For God sent not his Son into the world to condemn the world; but that the world through him might be saved. He that believeth on him is not condemned: but he that believeth not is condemned already, because he hath not believed in the name of the only begotten Son of God.*" This section of scripture tells us God's purpose for giving His son Jesus to the world. The world was in a bad condition. The world was overwrought with sin; the people were living for fleshly desires rather than for God's desires.

As a result of the world's conditions, God decided He would offer the perfect sacrifice that would save the world from being a place where people were lost and had no hope. He decided His own son could stand in proxy for the sin-filled world, taking all sin upon Himself. So Jesus came, born of a virgin, to save this dying world. He walked on this earth for 33 ½ years, doing the work of His Heavenly Father. At the appointed time, He died by way of crucifixion upon a cross at Calvary, on Golgotha's hill.

He shed His blood and died for you and for me. Because His blood was pure, it paid the penalty for all unrighteousness and gave those who believe in Him direct access to His father's throne.

Scripture tells us in Matthew 27:51 that the veil of the temple was ripped in two from top to bottom, at the moment that Jesus' spirit left His body. As a result of the veil's removal, we are no longer required to have a high priest make intercession for us. We, as the children of the Most High God, are able to approach the throne of God for ourselves, and Jesus sits on the right hand of the Father making intercession for us.

But what is even more miraculous than God offering His own son as the perfect sacrifice was the fact that when Jesus was placed in grave clothes and placed in a tomb, He only remained there until the third day. God would not have it that His son would remain in the heart of the earth forever. In order for people to believe in the awesome power of God and His dear son Jesus, a miracle had to be performed. So, on the third day, after Jesus died on the cross, He was resurrected, demonstrating the omnipotence of God. This very act was the act that would cause people to believe in a god that reigns supreme and holds the power of the universe in His very hands, a god that could save them from themselves.

Today, if you are an unbeliever, you can change your destiny. You can change where you will spend your eternity. Our Heavenly Father gives us the freedom of choice about how we want to live our life here on earth and how we want to spend eternity. In Deuteronomy

30:19, God boldly declares, "*I call heaven and earth to record this day against you, that I have set before you life and death, blessing and cursing: therefore choose life, that both thou and thy seed may live*."

So, dear friend what choice will you make today? Will you spend your eternity with the Creator or will you suffer Hell's eternal flames? Again, the choice is yours. Just as the men aboard the ship who were with Jonah became believers, you too can make a choice to accept the only one and true living God as your god.

If after reading the above passages, you have decided that you want to spend your eternity in Heaven with God, the creator, and His son Jesus, and the Holy Spirit, read through what has affectionately come to be known as the Roman's Road. This is the road to salvation. As you read through the scriptures that comprise the Roman's Road, you will also read the explanation for each scripture, so you will have clarity about what you are reading and confessing.

The Roman's Road to Salvation

The road to salvation begins with Romans 3:23, which declares, "*For all have sinned, and come short of the glory of God*." This scripture explains that everyone has come short of God's glory and needs redemption. Then, Romans 6:23a states, "*For the wages of sin is death*." Here, we learn that the consequence of living a life of sin is death. Everyone will experience physical death as a result of the sin committed in the garden of Eden, but those who commit themselves to a life of sin will suffer eternal damnation in the lake of fire (Rev. 19). Continue with the rest of verse 6:23 that says, "*but the gift of God is eternal life through Jesus Christ our Lord.*" There is an alternative to suffering eternal damnation. We can accept the gift of salvation by accepting Jesus as our personal Lord and Savior. Then, Romans 5:8 says, "*But God commendeth his love toward us, in that, while we were yet sinners, Christ died for us.*" We are able to receive the gift of salvation because Christ came to earth and shed His blood for us on the cross.

Continue to Romans 10: 9-10 which says, "*That if thou shalt confess with thy mouth the Lord Jesus, and shalt believe in thine heart that God hath raised him from the dead, thou shalt be saved. For with the heart man believeth unto righteousness; and with the mouth confession is made unto salvation.*" If we confess with our mouths that Jesus is the son of God, that He came and died for our sins, and that God raised Him from the dead, we will receive salvation.

Finish with Romans 10:13, which states, "*For whosoever shall call upon the name of the Lord shall be saved.*" Call upon the name of God by saying these words, **"Lord Jesus, come into my heart and save me, Lord. I believe that you are the Son of God who came and died on the cross for my sins. I believe that you rose from the grave. I also believe that you now sit in heaven on the right side of the Father, making intercession for me. I accept you as my Lord and my Savior."**

Now that you have confessed with your mouth that Jesus is the son of God and that He died for our sins and rose from the grave, **YOU ARE NOW SAVED!!!!** You will spend your eternity in heaven.

The next step is very important- you must find a Bible-based church that teaches the Word of God and confesses the Lord Jesus Christ to be the son of God. Don't delay. Do this immediately. Do not leave yourself open to the enemy. Get connected with the saints of the Most High God and keep yourself covered with the unspotted blood of the Lamb.

Here is my prayer for you.

Father God,

I thank you for the opportunity to minister your word to the unsaved, the unchurched, and the uncommitted. Father God, I pray now for the souls who have just received the gift of salvation. Lord Father, they have opened their hearts to you, and I know that you have received them into your kingdom and written their names in the Book of Life. Father God, I pray that you will touch their lives and show yourself mightily before them. Let their eyes be opened by the scales falling off, allowing them to see clearly.

Father God, I even pray for the backslider, those who have turned away from you after receiving the gift of salvation. You said in your Word that you desire that none would perish. So Lord, I send your Word to them right now, praying that they would confess the iniquity in their heart, repent, and turn from their evil ways, so that they may receive a life of abundance. You said in your Word in Matthew Chapter 14, that every knee shall bow before you and every tongue will confess that Jesus is Lord.

Father God, I pray now that we all come under subjection to your Word and that we will humbly submit our lives to you. I ask all these things in the name of my Lord and Savior Jesus Christ.
Amen, Amen, Amen!!!!

I will continue to pray for your success in your walk with God. Remember, this spiritual walk that you are about to embark on will not be an easy walk, but remember, the race is not given to the swift but to those who endure to the end.

Be blessed with heaven's best. I love you!

Bible Version Abbreviations

American Standard Version (ASV)
Amplified Bible (AMP)
English Standard Version (ESV)
Jubilee Bible 2000 (JB2000)
King James Version (KJV)
Lexham English Bible (LEB)
New American Standard Bible (NASB)
New International Version (NIV)
New King James Version (NKJV)
New Living Translation (NLT)
World English Bible (WEB)

ABOUT THE AUTHOR

Dr. Cassundra White-Elliott resides in California with her family, where as an English/Education professor, she teaches at various community colleges.

When writing, she composes with the direction of the Holy Spirit, in an effort to share with God's people all He has for them.

In addition to teaching and writing, Dr. Elliott also serves as an evangelistic teacher. She is also the founder of *International Women's Commission*, a ministry that serves the needs of the entire person, by attending to healing the mind, body, soul, and spirit.

Dr. Elliott holds a Ph.D. in Education, a Master's degree in English Composition, and a Bachelor's degree in Education.

Dr. Elliott is the founder and editor-in-chief for *Christian Inspiration* magazine, which covers topics germane to Christian living and the world at large.

Dr. Elliott is also the founder of CLF Publishing, LLC. For your publishing needs, go online to www.clfpublishing.org.

www.ingramcontent.com/pod-product-compliance
Lightning Source LLC
Chambersburg PA
CBHW070821100426
42813CB00003B/441